Merry-Go-Round Museum, Sandusky, Ohio

National Geographic's Driving Guides to America

Great Lakes

By Geoffrey O'Gara
Photographed by Layne Kennedy

Prepared by
The Book Division
National Geographic Society
Washington, D.C.

Credits

**National Geographic's
Driving Guides To America
Great Lakes**

By GEOFFREY O'GARA
Photographed by LAYNE KENNEDY

Published by
THE NATIONAL GEOGRAPHIC SOCIETY

Reg Murphy
  President and Chief Executive Officer
Gilbert M. Grosvenor
  Chairman of the Board
Nina D. Hoffman
  Senior Vice President

Prepared by The Book Division

William R. Gray
  Vice President and Director
Charles Kogod
  Assistant Director
Barbara A. Payne
  *Editorial Director and
  Managing Editor*

Driving Guides to America

Elizabeth L. Newhouse
  *Director of Travel Publishing
  and Series Editor*
Cinda Rose
  Art Director
Thomas B. Powell III
  Illustrations Editor
Caroline Hickey, Barbara A. Noe
  Senior Researchers
Carl Mehler
  Senior Map Editor and Designer

Staff for this book

Margaret Bowen
  Project Manager
Caroline Hickey
  Research Editor
Barbara A. Noe
  Associate Editor
Lyle Rosbotham
  Designer
Thomas B. Powell III
  Illustrations Editor
Carl Mehler
  Senior Map Editor and Designer

Thomas B. Blabey
Kristin M. Edmunds
Mark Fitzgerald
Sean M. Groom
Mary E. Jennings
Keith R. Moore
  Researchers

Lise Sajewski
  Editorial Consultant

Tracey M. Wood
  Map Production Manager

Thomas L. Gray, Joseph F. Ochlak
  Map Researchers
Michelle H. Picard, Louis J. Spirito,
and Mapping Specialists, Ltd.
  Map Production
Tibor G. Tóth
  Map Relief

Meredith C. Wilcox
  Illustrations Assistant
Richard S. Wain
  Production Project Manager
Lewis R. Bassford
  Production

Peggy Candore, Kevin G. Craig,
Dale M. Herring
  Staff Assistants

Michael H. Higgins, Justin Tejada
  Contributors

Susan Fels
  Indexer

**Manufacturing
and Quality Management**

George V. White, *Director*
John T. Dunn, *Associate Director*
Vincent P. Ryan, *Manager*

Cover: Pictured Rocks National Lakeshore,
Munising, Michigan
JOHN GERLACH/TONY STONE IMAGES

Previous pages: Freighter and Aerial Lift
Bridge, Duluth, Minnesota

Facing page: Abraham Lincoln's hat and
seat, Senate Chamber, Old State Capitol,
Springfield, Illinois

4

Contents

Upper Peninsula ★★
Sault Ste. Marie
ONTARIO
28
75
2
Mackinac I.
23
Lake Huron
31
Traverse City
Along Lake Michigan ★
75
MICHIGAN
Grand Rapids
96
27
Flint
69
Port Huron
Lansing ⭐
96
Detroit
Historic Passages
ONTARIO CANADA
Kalamazoo
Ann Arbor
Windsor
Lake Erie
UNITED STATES
PA.
94
69
23
90
Cleveland
20
80
90
80
South Bend
Fort Wayne
Cleveland Circle ⭐
Akron
Lakeshore and Farms
30
71
INDIANA
75
OHIO
65
Hoosierland ⭐
Columbus ⭐
70
Dayton
Indianapolis ⭐
23
Ohio's Heartland ⭐
77
37
74
50
Cincinnati
32
W. VA.
65
52
Portsmouth
150
New Albany
Southwest Corner
34
Ohio and Wabash

0   100 mi
0   150 km

*B*ack in the 19th century, according to family lore, my great-great-grandmother told her two sons to travel north from their home in Madison, Wisconsin, and dig for iron ore on a worthless parcel of land near the Michigan border. She was an iron-willed woman who often claimed divine inspiration, and her sons did as they were told. Soon they were in the mining business, and prospering.

Costumed interpreters, Old World Wisconsin

Back then the Great Lakes region was callow and raw, littered with mines and logging camps and new farms, washed over by a great tide of immigrant humanity. Today, the pace of development has slowed, and when I express my interest in mining on Michigan's Upper Peninsula, my hosts send me to a museum. How rapidly we become history!

Of course there are still operating mines, and Buicks rolling off assembly lines, and full grain silos in the port cities. Industry is one of the attractions—along with natural beauty and history—that draws travelers here. In the far north you can take a rattling elevator down a mineshaft, watch "living history" voyageurs paddle ashore at Old Fort William, or do your own canoeing in the Boundary Waters. In the hilly Appalachian country south of the lakes, you can walk among ghosts at the ancient Serpent Mound, or sip the local vintages at an Indiana winery.

Just how abruptly the travel season ends in the northern climes of the Great Lakes I found out last year, when I arrived at Mackinac Island on Labor Day. The island is a mother lode of history and scenery, but I discovered to my chagrin that many sites would shut down for the season at 4 p.m. that day. No motorized vehicles are allowed, so I rented a bicycle and shot off to circumnavigate the island. That evening, when I pedaled sweaty and disheveled up the last steep hill to the majestic Grand Hotel, no amount of pleading could get me in the dining room.

Perhaps I should have put my nose in the air and told them that my great-grandfather used to come here, when he was an iron baron on the Upper Peninsula (though I have no idea if he did). Instead, I coasted down the hill and waded into Lake Superior up to my knees. No baron or big shot, I was just a drop of water in a huge sea of history, humanity, and natural beauty pooling here at the heart of America. Come and get your feet wet.

GEOFFREY O'GARA

8

Lake Effect

It's November, and you wake up to a crisp morning of wispy clouds in Princeton, Ill., and decide to drive up to Lake Michigan for a hike in the Indiana dunes. Suddenly, about 30 miles from the lake, you enter a meteorological twilight zone: Blue sky turns to blizzard, cars perform icy pirouettes, and the world is erased by a blinding swirl of wet snow. Welcome to the "lake effect," a cocktail of dry cold Canadian air and warm lake water, served shaken, not stirred. Moisture rises from the warmer lakes, and the party is on (most often in late fall and early winter). Check the weather reports.

About the Guides

*N*ATIONAL GEOGRAPHIC'S DRIVING GUIDES TO AMERICA invite you on memorable road trips through the United States and Canada. Intended both as travel planners and companions, each volume guides you on pre-planned tours over a wide variety of terrain to the best places to see and things to do. The authors, expert regional travel writers, star-rate (from none to two ★★) the drives and points of interest to make sure you don't miss their favorites.

Clifty Falls State Park, Madison, Indiana

All distances and drive times are approximate (if you linger, as you should, plan on considerably more time). Recommended seasons are the best times to go, but roads and sites are open all year unless otherwise noted. Besides the stated days of operation, many sites close on national holidays. For the most up-to-date site information, it's best to call ahead when possible.

Then, with this book and a road map, set off on your adventure through this awesomely beautiful land.

9

MAP KEY and ABBREVIATIONS

Military Reservation
National Lakeshore .... N.L.
National Park .... N.P.
National Recreation Area .... N.R.A.
National Scenic Riverway

National Forest .... NAT. FOR., N.F.
State Forest .... S.F.
Wilderness Area

National Wildlife and Fish Refuge
National Wildlife Refuge .... N.W.R.

Provincial Park
State Fish and Wildlife Area .... S.F.W.A.
State Natural Area .... S.N.A.
State Park .... S.P.
State Recreation Area .... S.R.A.
Wildlife Area

Indian Reservation .... I.R.

ADDITIONAL ABBREVIATIONS

A.F.B.	*Air Force Base*
Cr., CR.	*Creek*
Fk.	*Fork*
Hbr.	*Harbor*
I.	*Island*
I & M	*Illinois and Michigan*
L.	*Lake*
Mt., MT.	*Mount, Mountain*
NAT.	*National*
NAT. MEM.	*National Memorial*
N.E.R.R.	*National Estuarine Research Reserve*
N.H.P.	*National Historical Park*
N.S.T.	*National Scenic Trail*
R.	*River*
S.H.S.	*State Historic Site*
S.H.P.	*State Historic Park*
S. MEM.	*State Memorial*
S.N.P.	*State Nature Preserve*
St.-e., ST.	*Saint-e*

Featured Drive

Interstate Highway
(94)

U.S. Federal Highway
(50)

State Road
(66)

Trans-Canada Highway
(1)

Principal Canadian Highway
MAJOR (2) MINOR

County, Local, or Other Road
(7)

Trail

State or National Border

Ferry
FEATURED   OTHER

Canal
IN USE   ABANDONED

National Forest Boundary

■ Point of Interest   ✪ State Capital

POPULATION

● **Milwaukee**   500,000 and over
● **South Bend**   50,000 to under 500,000
● Bainbridge   under 50,000

Chicago and West★★

● **500 miles** ● **6 to 7 days** ● **Year-round**

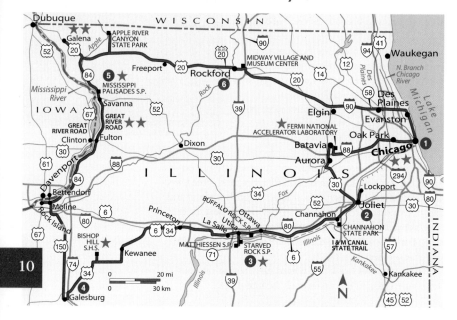

Taking its name from an Indian word for the wild onions growing along the marshy Lake Michigan shore, Chicago itself grew with abandon in the 19th century, as hundreds of thousands of people streamed in. First a gateway to the vast interior of the new nation, it became a hub for midwestern commerce and paraded its prosperity with a jaunt that was at once boastful and exhilarating.

The Windy City—a reference to the boasting, not the weather—is the portal for this ramble around northern Illinois. The route goes west through old canal towns and natural preserves, journeying all the way west to the busy Quad Cities on the Mississippi River. From Rock Island you follow the great river north to the charming, steep streets of historic Galena, then cross the state east to the Lake Michigan shore and, once again, the "city of big shoulders."

That's what poet Carl Sandburg called ❶ **Chicago**★★ *(Convention & Tourism Bureau 312-567-8500)* because he, like many others, thought of the city almost as if it were a person, loved for its outsized flaws as much for its graces. From the downtown high-rises to the bohemian world of Old Town, those shoulders carry a diverse load of people, drawn from all over the country and the world. It is a world-class commercial center, and a way station for trainloads of grain, freighters heavy with coal, and trucks loaded with manufactured goods. But Chicago has a vibrancy much greater than the frizzle of its commerce. No other American cities but New York and Los Angeles can match its cultural diversity and arts scene, and its history, young though it is by world standards, is beautifully etched in its architecture.

For the outstanding city design we can apparently thank a cow, which stands accused of kicking over a lantern in Patrick O'Leary's barn one October night in 1871. The largely wooden city was decimated by a roaring fire, the heat of which could be felt across the lake in Holland, Michigan. From that tragedy, a better planned,

Enjoying Chicago's architecture from the Chicago River

better working, and immensely confident city arose, and Chicago became a showcase for skyscrapers and urban design. Even the debris from the fire was a plus: It was shoved behind a lakeside breakwater, and became the foundation of what's now Grant Park.

Not a bad place to start: The parks that line much of Chicago's lakeshore make this a particularly livable city, with leaf, lawn, and sand buffering the cityscape. Grant and Jackson Parks on the city's south side, and Lincoln Park on the north side also contain world-class museums, science centers, a zoo, and an aquarium. You might want to park the car and go by foot or public transportation.

The Grant Park museums alone are worth a week's

time—for that matter, you could spend hours gawking at just one painting, Georges Seurat's pointillist "Sunday Afternoon on the Island of La Grande Jatte," at the **Art Institute of Chicago**★★ *(Michigan Ave. and Adams St. 312-443-3600. Donation)*. Walk past the institute's sentry lions and into a den of antiquity, stocked from huge collections of ancient and international art ranging from 3000 B.C. to present day. In the vast museum's quieter corners, you'll discover fascinating exhibits of contemporary urban photography, architectural drawings, and ornamentation from destroyed Chicago buildings. Also in Grant Park looms the zodiac-shape **Adler Planetarium and Astronomy Museum** *(1300 S. Lake Shore Dr. 312-322-0300. Adm. fee)*, where you can see the galaxies up close and tour exhibits on space exploration; the enormous **John G. Shedd Aquarium** *(1200 S. Lake Shore Dr. 312-939-2438. Adm. fee)*, which offers dolphin and whale shows; and the **Field Museum**★ *(Roosevelt Rd. and Lake Shore Dr. 312-922-9410. Adm. fee)*, whose exhibits are culled from more than 19 million artifacts ranging from dinosaur bones to Native American crafts.

Farther south along the lake is the site of the 1893 World's Columbian Exposition, the 400-year celebration of the Europeans' discovery of America. The fair's Palace of Fine Arts became the 15-acre **Museum of Science and Industry**★ *(57th St. and Lake Shore Dr. 773-684-1414. Adm. fee)*, where you can walk through a 16-foot-high human heart and visit an underground coal mine.

Gustav Caillebotte's "Paris Street; Rainy Day," Art Institute of Chicago

Moving north along the lakeshore brings you to the glittering **Navy Pier** *(600 E. Grand Ave. 312-595-PIER or 800-595-PIER)* jutting out into the lake between Grant and Lincoln Parks at the foot of the downtown area. The 1916 pier has been modernized as a shopping and entertainment center featuring a towering Ferris wheel, IMAX 3-D theater, and a dock where you can hook up with sightseeing boats, both power and sail. Newly moved to the pier is the Chicago Academy of Sciences' **Nature Museum**★ *(435 E. Illinois St., 3rd level. 773-871-2668. Adm.*

12

fee), where kids can build a kite or get muddy routing a river on the sand-filled Stream Table. At Lincoln Park's south end awaits the **Chicago Historical Society** *(Clark St. and North Ave. 312-642-4600. Adm. fee),* with permanent exhibits on Chicago history, some key historic documents including a first printing of the Bill of Rights, and a rich variety of lectures and films. The society provides walking and bus tours of the city; reservations are required.

Beluga whale performing at the John G. Shedd Aquarium, Chicago

13

If you want to get an overview of the city before you start wandering its streets— and a view as well of the lake and bordering states—levitate to the 1,353-foot Sky- deck, on the 103rd floor of the rabbit-eared **Sears Tower** *(233 S. Wacker Dr., entrance on Jackson Blvd. 312-875-9696. Adm. fee).* Sears is the world's third tallest building, but it takes only 70 seconds for the elevators to climb its 110 stories. Some prefer the view from the slightly lower elevation of the 100-story **John Hancock Center** *(875 N. Michigan Ave. 312-751-3681 or 888-875-8439. Adm. fee),* where you can tilt your glass in the Signature Lounge on the 96th floor while gazing at the Loop or the lake, or visit the 94th-floor observatory.

The **Loop** is the core of the city, circled by ribbons of cable car tracks and now by the tracks of the "El" (elevated trains). A virtual history of modern urban architecture, as well as fine monumental art, can be seen on a fairly short Loop walking tour. There are other tour options—on the water, by bus, even by plane. Tour information is available at one of two Visitor Centers: at the **Historic Water Tower** *(800 N. Michigan Ave. 312-744-6630),* a miniature Gothic castle that hides a 140-foot pipe in its limestone tower, one of two buildings to survive the 1871 fire; or at the **Chicago Cultural Center** *(78 E. Washington St. 312-744-6630),* a busy 1897 beaux arts building where the city mounts exhibits and stages free concerts. At the Visitor Centers you can pick up tickets during the summer for a free Saturday afternoon guided tour on the city's "El," or rent "Audio Architecture," an inexpensive 90-minute self-guided tour with tape player and map.

The best resource for anyone interested in urban design is the **Chicago Architecture Foundation Shop and Tour Center** ★ ★ *(224 S. Michigan Ave. 312-922-8687. Fee for tours. Reservations required for bus tours and river cruises).* The foundation's docents lead visitors on downtown bus and walking tours, and also on cruises that glide beneath the Chicago River's many bridges for a unique look at landmark buildings.

Architectural tastes vary, but there are several can't-miss structures worth seeing on your own or by tour. Shoppers can mask their passion for purchase behind a veneer of historical curiosity at two magnificent turn-of-the-century department stores: **Carson Pirie Scott** ★ *(1 S. State St. 312-641-7000),* an 1899 Louis Sullivan masterpiece with cast-iron floral ornaments, and **Marshall Field's** *(835 N. Michigan Ave. 312-335-7700),* with its big atrium and iron fountain in the midst of 73 acres of floor space. Both stores have been renovated extensively and feature specialty shops for the most au courant tastes.

A few blocks away stands the 1930 art deco **Chicago Board of Trade** ★ *(141 W. Jackson Blvd. 312-435-3590. Mon.-Fri.),* housing the oldest and largest futures exchanges. Traders jam together in a frenzied crush of buying and selling that may look like a deranged rugby match from the gallery. In fact, fortunes are being made and lost with the wave of a frantic hand.

North of the Michigan Avenue Bridge rise two 1920s gems, the **Wrigley Building** *(400 N. Michigan Ave.),* a white sugar confection of terra-cotta, and the 1922 **Tribune Tower** *(435 N. Michigan Ave.),* a mammoth Gothic structure with flying buttresses and imbedded stones stolen from the

Playing volleyball on a Lake Michigan beach

Parthenon and the Egyptian Pyramids by the newspaper's reporters. Ludwig Mies van der Rohe brought Chicago into the modern era with designs such as the **Federal Center** *(219 S. Dearborn St.),* where solid slabs of Bauhaus are offset by Alexander Calder's curvaceous "Flamingo" sculpture.

Calder's sculpture is only one of many monumental outdoor artworks that decorate the city. The artists' roster is a who's who of 20th-century greats: There are Picasso's untitled 1967 50-foot-tall sculpture at **Richard J. Daley Civic Center Plaza** *(50 W. Washington Blvd.)*, a popular site for public demonstrations; Marc Chagall's huge mosaic, "The Four Seasons," at the **First National Plaza** *(Dearborn and Monroe Sts.)*; Claes Oldenburg's amusing 100-foot "Bat-column" at the **Harold Washington SSA Building Plaza** *(600 W. Madison St.)*; and many others, described in a guide available at the Visitor Centers.

A few other downtown attractions shouldn't be missed. The **Chicago Athenaeum** *(6 N. Michigan Ave. 312-251-0175. Closed Mon.; donation)* features fascinating displays on architecture and industrial design from radios to ice-cream scoops; and the spacious new **Museum of Contemporary Art**★★ *(220 E. Chicago Ave. 312-280-2660. Closed Mon.)* offers airy exhibit areas for modern sculpture and paintings.

In the evening, Chicago offers the unquenchable variety you would expect in a cosmopolitan city, from the **Chicago Symphony** *(220 S. Michigan Ave. 312-294-3000. Adm. fee)* to the comedy club **Second City** *(1616 N. Wells St. 312-337-3992. Adm. fee)* to the world-champion **Chicago Bulls** *(United Center, 1901 W. Madison St. 312-455-4500. Adm. fee)* during basketball season. What Chicago has that no other city can match—well, besides Michael Jordan—is a lineup of blues

Sears Tower

clubs that define the idiom. A good place to start is **Buddy Guy's Legends**★ *(745 S. Wabash Ave. 312-427-1190. Adm. fee)*, where you may get lucky and find the guitar giant himself jamming with his old harmonica-mate, Junior Wells.

Best to get back in the car for visits to the city's fringes. On the South Side you can tour the Gothic Revival buildings of the **University of Chicago** *(1212 E. 59th St. 773-702-8374)*, including the **Rockefeller Memorial Chapel** *(5850 S. Woodlawn Ave. 773-702-9292. Call for carillon concert schedule)*, a structure designed by Bertram Good-hue. Also on campus is the **Robie House** *(5757 S. Woodlawn Ave. 773-702-2150. Adm. fee)*, one of Frank

Lloyd Wright's Prairie School designs.

Some of Wright's finest work can be found in the west Chicago suburb of **Oak Park** *(Visitors Bureau 708-524-7800)*. The architect perfected the Prairie School style in more than twenty Oak Park residences, many of them seen on a neighborhood walking tour with audiotapes provided by the **Frank Lloyd Wright Home and Studio** ★★ *(951 Chicago Ave. 708-848-1978. Adm. fee)*. Also on the route is the Wright-designed **Unity Temple** *(875 Lake St. 708-383-8873. Guided tours Mem. Day–Labor Day Sat.-Sun.; adm. fee for tour)*, a 1909 poured-concrete building of massive simplicity. Guided tours of Wright's house and studio feature an octagonal-roofed structure on a square base, a chil-

Moore-Dugal Residence, designed by Frank Lloyd Wright, Oak Park

16

dren's playroom with a barrel-vaulted ceiling, and panel dividers that indicate Wright, at only 22, was already influenced by Japanese design.

Wright's celebrity in Oak Park is oddly paired with author Ernest Hemingway, who was born here in 1899. The **Ernest Hemingway Museum** *(200 N. Oak Park Ave. 708-848-2222. Fri.-Sun.; adm. fee)*, a block from his actual birthplace at 339 N. Oak Park Avenue, exhibits the writer's early scribblings and memorabilia.

West of Oak Park in **Batavia,** you can take a free tour of the fastest energy-particle accelerator in the world at the **Fermi National Accelerator Laboratory** ★ *(Kirk Rd. and Pine St. 630-840-3351. Call for tour information)*. The protons whiz around at nearly the speed of light in a helium-cooled tube that encircles a peaceful acreage of experimentally restored prairie, complete with hiking and biking trails.

In nearby **Aurora,** the *Hollywood Casino* *(1 New York St. Bridge. 630-801-1234 or 800-888-7777)* follows the letter of Illinois gambling laws by conducting its business in faux riverboats that cast off and go nowhere but about 50 feet from the dock.

Drive south to ❷ **Joliet** and its entertainment palaces old and new: The **Rialto Square Theater** *(102 N. Chicago St. 815-726-6600. Adm. fee)* was a classic vaudeville and movie house, and still stages extravaganzas behind its six-story facade of glorious ornamental terra-cotta, tile, and gild; two blocks away on the river, you'll find casinos housed in pale imitations of the great riverboats of old, the **Empress Casino Joliet** *(2300 Empress Dr. 708-345-6789 or 888-4EMPRESS)* and **Harrah's Joliet Casino** *(151 N. Joliet St. 815-740-7800 or 800-HARRAHS)*.

A quick jaunt north on Ill. 171 brings you to **Lockport** *(Chamber of Commerce 815-838-3357)*, the headquarters for the Illinois & Michigan (I&M) Canal, a man-made waterway that rose through a series of locks to connect the Des Plaines and Chicago Rivers, linking the Great Lakes to the Mississippi River system in the 1840s. Exhibits in the **Illinois & Michigan Canal Museum** *(803 S. State St. 815-838-5080)* describe the building of the canal and its commercial significance. Down along the canal itself, you can stroll through a village of pioneer buildings made of hand-hewn logs.

The drive now follows the 96-mile I&M Canal route west. Barges have not floated through the canal's 15 locks since 1933, but the towpaths are busy with walkers and bicyclists, and wayside signs explain what life was like here 150 years ago. Lengthy portions of the towpaths form the **I&M Canal State Trail** *(For maps and information call 815-942-0796)* beginning at **Channahon State Park** *(Canal St., Channahon. 815-467-4271)*, a shady enclave featuring two of the canal's locks and a lock-tender's house. The trail runs 60 miles to La Salle, with many accesses along the way. Among them awaits **Buffalo Rock State Park** *(Dee Bennett Rd. 815-433-2220)*, featuring five mound sculptures made in the 1980s by reclaiming strip-mine

Inside *Harrah's Joliet Casino*

17

spoil piles that had blighted the landscape since the 1930s. You can hike among the "Effigy Tumuli," shaped in the style of Indian burial mounds to resemble creatures including frogs and water striders.

Two miles west at the **Illinois Waterway Visitor Center** *(Dee Bennett Rd. 815-667-4054)*, you can learn about locks and dams and watch them at work. You also get a good view of 2,630-acre ❸ **Starved Rock State Park**★

(1 mile S of Utica, on Ill. 178. 815-667-4726), across the river. The park is centered around a sandstone prominence where an 18th-century band of Illiniwek starved to death

while besieged by enemies below. Many today are fed in its 1930s lodge and restaurant, and hiking trails wind along the river and into deep, craggy canyons. South on Ill. 178 you'll find **Matthiessen State Park** *(815-667-4868)*—more bluffs and canyons and fewer people.

Religious dissidents from Sweden built a utopian community on the Illinois plains in the 1840s, and today the wide, peaceful

Ulysses S. Grant Home State Historic Site, Galena

18

streets and sturdy buildings of **Bishop Hill State Historic Site** ★ *(N of US 34. 309-927-3345. Donation)* still reflect the simplicity and rigor that made it a success. The town is now a mixture of craft shops and restored historical sites, including the 1848 church, with displays reflecting the beliefs of leader Erik Jansson and his flock.

Among the Swedish immigrants who settled in central Illinois was a couple named Sandburg, whose child Carl became a renowned poet and biographer of Abraham Lincoln. Sandburg's ashes are buried behind his family's three-room cottage in ❹ **Galesburg,** at the **Carl Sandburg State Historic Site** *(331 E. 3rd St. 309-342-2361. Donation)*. The house contains family furnishings, and the Visitor Center focuses on Sandburg's life and work.

The route turns north to meet the Mississippi River at the **Quad Cities** *(Visitors Bureau 309-788-7800 or 800-747-7800)*, with Moline and Rock Island on the Illinois bank and Davenport and Bettendorf on the Iowa side. The economies of these towns grew around two farm implement dealers, John Deere and International Harvester. Deere was a blacksmith turned industrialist whose self-scouring steel plow furrowed the plains. At Deere & Company's beautifully landscaped, modern **World Headquarters** *(John Deere Rd., 7 miles SE of Moline. 309-765-4793)* you can climb on tractors of all sizes and see artifacts of old-time farming. In downtown Moline, there are more extensive displays on how food gets from the seed to the plate at the new **John Deere Pavilion** *(River Dr. 309-765-1000)*—part of a complex on the river that

offers shopping, restaurants, and hotels.

Before there were tractors, there were the Sauk and Fox tribes, who rebelled when settlers plowed up their burial grounds. The story of the Black Hawk War of 1832, and the Indian way of life before Europeans came, is told at the **John Hauberg Indian Museum** *(1510 46th St., Rock Island. 309-788-9536. Closed Mon.-Tues. Dec.-Feb.; donation),* on a bluff above the Rock River in **Blackhawk State Historic Site.**

The U.S. Army makes artillery guns, M-9 pistols, and other armaments on Arsenal Island in the Mississippi River. **Rock Island Arsenal Museum** *(Bldg. 60. 309-782-5021)* displays everything from Indian war flintlocks to captured Iraqi assault rifles. Explore the island and you'll come upon a meadow of plain grave markers surrounded by cannons: the cemetery where nearly 2,000 Confederate soldiers and 125 Union guards were laid to rest during the island's years as a Civil War prison.

Like so many other river towns, the Quad Cities now host gambling boats, three at last count, which cast off for gaming on the not-so-high seas. Not all boats on the river are crammed with one-armed bandits, though, and this is one of the most rewarding stretches of the great river for sight-seeing. Driving north on Ill. 84 and US 20—along the **Great River Road**★★—you'll see barges, fishing boats, and a rare canoe wandering the broad river, which braids around an island now and then, and undercuts tall wooded bluffs along the shore. At ❺ **Mississippi Palisades State Park**★ *(4577 Ill. 84, Savanna. 815-273-2731),* trails take you right to the edge of these cliffs for breathtaking views.

Well before most American towns realized the appetite travelers have for history, **Galena**★★ *(Visitors Bureau 815-777-0203 or 800-747-9377)* had begun preserving and publicizing its 19th-century look. It comes by its historical buildings honestly. Lead mining created wealth in Galena in the 1820s—it became the biggest river port north of St. Louis, and soon its hills were dotted with opulent buildings. River silt and the decline of the mines quieted the commerce long ago, but today the charm of its steep, narrow streets and fine old architecture lures crowds. The **Old Market House State Historic Site** *(123 N. Commerce St. 815-777-2570. Thurs.-Mon.; donation)* offers information about Galena's sights, a well-preserved corner of a general store, and architecture and history displays. More in-depth exhibits are found up the hill at the **Galena/Jo Daviess County History Museum** *(211 S. Bench St. 815-777-9129. Adm. fee).* And the Italianate 1857 **Belvedere**

Early Melting Pot

The Illinois Historic Preservation Agency recently finished excavating a site near Starved Rock that should fill a missing link in the region's history from the time French missionary Jacques Marquette first made contact with a band of Illiniwek people in 1675. Thriving in the 1680s and 1690s, the Starved Rock village consisted of 400 cabins, which the French called the Grand Village of the Illinois. The band was later decimated by marauding Iroquois and disease. Archaeological digs have revealed the boundaries of the Grand Village and uncovered storage pits, bone antler ornaments, and artifacts from the brief era of assimilation, including brass kettles and other European implements. Officials say that when funding is available, the site will be developed and opened to visitors.

19

Mansion *(1008 Park Ave. 815-777-0747. Adm. fee)* lavishly shows off a steamboat magnate's wealth in its 22 rooms.

One Galena resident was neither rich nor well known when he left to serve the Union in the Civil War, but when Ulysses S. Grant returned, proud locals gave him a handsome brick home. The Grants lived in what is now the **Ulysses S. Grant Home State Historic Site** *(500 Bouthillier St. 815-777-0248. Donation)* periodically after the war until 1881.

Hilly Galena is in part of what geologists call the "driftless area"—country that escaped the scouring, flattening effects of ice age glaciers. To explore these steep hills and canyons, proceed east on US 20 and north on N. Canyon Park Road to **Apple River Canyon State Park** *(815-745-3302. Park office open Mon.-Fri.)* and hike along the river.

Heading back toward Chicago, urban reentry begins in ❻ **Rockford** *(Visitors Bureau 815-963-8111 or 800-521-0849)*. Here, **Midway Village and Museum Center** *(6799 Guildford Rd. 815-397-9112. Adm. fee)* re-creates a village of a century ago. At the **Discovery Center** *(711 N. Main St. 815-963-6769. June-Aug. daily, Sept.-May Tues.-Sun.; adm. fee)* computers and giant magnets make science fun.

Farm-dotted hills around Galena

Farther east, pick up I-90 to **Des Plaines,** where the golden arches still advertise a 15-cent burger at the **McDonald's Museum** *(400 Lee St. 847-297-5022)*. From here, follow Ill. 58 to **Evanston,** home of **Northwestern University** *(Admissions Office, 1967 Sheridan Rd. 847-491-7271)* and its various gardens and sculpture. The historical society is lodged in the 1894 **Charles Gates Dawes House** *(225 Greenwood St. 847-475-3410. Adm. fee)*, where Calvin Coolidge's vice president once lived. Finally, the **Grosse Point Lighthouse and Lakefront** ★ *(2601 Sheridan Rd. 847-328-6961. June-Sept. Sat.-Sun.; adm. fee)* has nice stretches of beach, historical buildings, and the yellow lighthouse tower, erected in 1873 and topped by a beacon that still works. Return to Chicago via US 41.

Lincoln Country★

● **400 miles** ● **3 to 4 days** ● **Year-round**

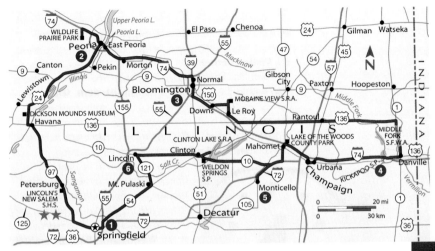

Chicago may be the nerve center of the Great Lakes region, but that does not make it the heart of Illinois. A search for the state's essential character takes you mid-state, to the rolling farmlands and smaller cities such as Springfield, Peoria, and Champaign-Urbana. It's here that you find the great expanses of cornfields, the seat of government, and the historic footsteps of Abraham Lincoln, America's most revered President.

The tour begins in Springfield, Illinois's capital and the town where Lincoln first flourished as a lawyer and legislator. The route travels north to the meandering Illinois River and Peoria, the embodiment of middle America to many, and then east to Bloomington and Champaign. The drive is capped with a visit to the town of Lincoln, home of a museum devoted to "honest Abe."

Old State Capitol, Springfield

❶ **Springfield** (*Convention & Visitors Bureau 217-789-2360 or 800-545-7300*), the route's starting point, is fairly bursting with Lincolniana. It was here, in 1837, that 28-year-old Lincoln came—with all his possessions stuffed in two saddlebags. His law career thrived in Springfield, where he also met his wife and bought a house. Since then the city has grown into a robust metropolis. If you visit the **Illinois State Capitol** *(2nd and Capitol Sts. 217-782-2099)* during a legislative session, you can watch Lincoln's successors from the balcony (though he served in the Old State Capitol). There are guided tours of the building, and behind the capitol to the west is a **Visitor Center** *(225 S. College St. 217-524-6620. Mon.-Sat.)* with information about the state and its government. Also within this complex is the **Illinois State Museum** *(Spring and Edwards Sts. 217-782-7386),* with displays on Illinois wildlife back to the age of the mastodons, as well as Indian cultures of the region, decorative arts from several centuries, and a Discovery Room for children.

The fecund soil of central Illinois produces more than corn: Beautiful roses, orchids, and poinsettias are on display in formal gardens and in a domed conservatory at the **Washington Park Botanical Garden** *(1740 W. Fayette Ave. 217-782-6776).*

Another site worth noting in Springfield is the **Dana-Thomas House**★★ *(301 E. Lawrence Ave. 217-782-6772; Wed.-Sun.; adm. fee),* a Victorian house remodeled by Frank Lloyd Wright into a double cruciform floor plan with 16 different levels. Completed in 1904, with art glass windows in butterfly and sumac patterns, it's one of the finest examples of Wright's prairie-style houses.

Now segue to the Lincoln sites and artifacts that are everywhere in this city the nation's 16th President

Lincoln memorabilia, Old State Capitol

so loved. Best to begin at the **Old State Capitol**★ *(5th and Adams Sts. 217-785-7961. Donation),* where Lincoln served a term in the legislature. Within the cupola-domed limestone building are exhibits on early Illinois government and 19th-century furnishings. Lincoln tried cases before the state supreme court here, and delivered his famed 1858 speech on the extension of slavery, declaring, "A house divided against itself cannot stand...." It was also here that he lay in state, in the Hall of Representatives.

Next visit the **Lincoln-Herndon Law Offices State Historic Site** *(6th and Adams Sts. 217-785-7289. Donation),* restored with period furnishings. Here Lincoln had the irritating habit of reading the newspaper aloud. While

making his rounds, he often tucked important legal papers under his stovepipe hat—this resulted in many a lost document. To see the pew where Lincoln, Mary Todd, and their sons worshiped, visit the **First Presbyterian Church** *(321 S. 7th St. 217-528-4311. June-Sept. Mon.-Fri.).*

The most intimate connection to Lincoln, though, is made with a visit to the **Lincoln Home National Historic Site**★★ *(Visitor Center, 426 S. 7th St. 217-492-4241 ext. 221; free with ticket),* which stands in a shady four-block neighborhood that has been closed to vehicles and restored to the look and feel of the 1860s. Though some might question Mary Todd Lincoln's taste in carpet and wallpaper—authentic re-creations, guides say—you'll feel like part of the family as docents tell stories inside the house. Imagine the lanky Lincoln stretching out on the floor of the informal parlor (the chairs were too small).

Lincoln's body, along with Mary and three of their sons, lies beneath an obelisk monument at the **Lincoln Tomb State Historic Site** *(Oak Ridge Cemetery, 1500 Monument Ave. 217-782-2717).* Around the tomb are various statues, including a Lincoln bust by Gutzon Borglum (of Mount Rushmore fame) and a bronze model of the seated President from the Lincoln Memorial in Washington, D.C. In 1876 thieves attempted to kidnap Lincoln's body for ransom, but were caught before they completed the act.

The route goes northwest from Springfield on Ill. 97, to explore Lincoln's young adulthood at **Lincoln's New Salem State Historic Site**★★ *(Ill. 97. 217-632-4000. Donation),* the 600-acre park includes a restoration of the village where 21-year-old Abe arrived poling a flatboat. He stayed to try his hand at shopkeeping and surveying, and studied law by candlelight. Once you're past the modern Visitor Center, the log village smells of hearth fires and leafy oaks. Interpreters in period dress demonstrate skills at the blacksmith forge, the cooper shop, and the gristmill, and historical dramas are staged at the amphitheater on summer weekends *(217-632-5440 or 800-710-9290. June-Aug.; adm. fee).* Nearby a small riverboat, the ***Talisman*** *(Ill. 97, 2.5 miles S of Petersburg. 217-632-2219. May–Labor Day daily, Labor Day–Oct. weekends; fare),* offers 45-minute narrated rides on the Sangamon River; Lincoln himself patented a device in 1849 to make navigation easier on shallow rivers such as the Sangamon.

For a change of pace, drive farther north on Ill. 97, to one of the region's largest prehistoric burial grounds. Located along the banks of the Illinois River, the **Rockwell Mound** *(500 N. Orange St., Havana)* dates from

Lincoln Lore

Abraham Lincoln's reputation for wit and eloquence first came to national attention in his seven debates with Stephen A. Douglas during their 1858 U.S. Senate race. The debates, running for hours, centered on the hot-button issue of the day, slavery, with Douglas arguing to let each state decide, and Lincoln declaring, "This government cannot endure permanently half slave and half free." After hearing Douglas address a crowd in Clinton, Lincoln reputedly said, "You can fool all of the people some of the time; and some of the people all of the time; but you can not fool all the people all of the time." Remembering such ringing phrases, people often forget the context: Lincoln was denying Douglas's charge that he believed in political equality for blacks—not exactly his finest moment. Nor do many of us remember the outcome of the Senate race: Lincoln lost. But when he ran for President two years later, Douglas endorsed him.

23

A.D. 300. Various artifacts, art, and archaeology related to the Indians, who occupied this region over a 12,000-year period, are displayed at the **Dickson Mounds Museum** *(10956 N. Dickson Mounds Rd., Lewistown. 309-547-3721)*.

The Illinois River widens to form two lakes at ❷ **Peoria** *(Convention & Visitors Bureau, 403 N.E. Jefferson St. 309-676-0303 or 800-747-0302)*, which made it an attractive home first to Indians and later to French explorers, who in 1680 built **Fort Crevecoeur** *(508 Scenic Park Dr. 309-694-3193)*. The park today includes a reproduction of the fort, an Indian village, a museum, and a playground. In September, a 17th-century rendezvous of latter-day Indians and French traders is staged. The oldest residence in Peoria is the **John C. Flanagan House** *(942 N.E. Glen Oak Ave. 309-674-1921. By appt.; adm. fee)*, an early 1840s brick house that features exhibits on Peoria life in the 19th century. Using a guide provided by the Convention & Visitors Bureau, take a walk in the **West Bluff Historic District** *(Moss and High Sts.)*, where you'll see an amazing concentration of old architectural styles. Several of the buildings beg for restoration, but you can still appreciate the faded majesty of the Queen Anne mansion at 429 High Street, with its onion-dome belvedere; and the 1868 **Pettengill-Morron House** *(1212 W. Moss St. 309-674-4745. By appt.; adm. fee)*, furnished in the post-Civil War period.

Prehistoric artifacts, Dickson Mounds Museum

Many river towns these days offer a nostalgic spin on a stern-wheeler. The smallish ***Spirit of Peoria*** *(100 N.E. Constitution and Main Sts., at the river. 309-699-7232. Wed., Fri., and Sun.; fare)* cruises from the Landing, where there is a stage and various restaurants. Finally, four acres of gardens make **George Luthy Memorial Botanical Gardens** *(2218 N. Prospect Rd. 309-686-3362. Donation)* worth a stop.

Before crossing the river to East Peoria, head northwest to the **Wildlife Prairie Park** *(3826 N. Taylor Rd., Kickapoo/Edwards exit off I-74. 309-676-0998. Closed mid-Dec.–mid-March; adm. fee)*, which goes back in time to the Illinois prairie of a few centuries ago, replete with bison, bald eagles, and black bears. You can hike or ride a train to view the animals and to visit a pioneer farmstead.

Across the Illinois is East Peoria and the ***Par-A-Dice***

(21 Blackjack Blvd. 309-694-5900 or 800-847-7117. Adm. fee).
Sometimes this sleek gambling boat casts off and sometimes it doesn't, depending on the weather. It hardly mat-
ters to the crowds, who lose themselves in several decks
of gaming tables and slot machines.

The route along I-74 follows the corn belt east to
❸ **Bloomington** *(Convention & Visitors Bureau 309-829-
1641 or 800-433-8226),* linked inevitably to Abraham Lincoln, whose key presidential campaign strategist lived
here. Lincoln showed his appreciation by appointing
David Davis to the U.S. Supreme Court. In the 1870s, the
Bloomington lawyer built the mansard-roofed, yellow-
brick **David Davis Mansion State Historic Site** ★ *(1000 E.
Monroe St. 309-828-1084. Thurs.-Mon.; donation).* It stands
alone at the center of a grassy block, so you can walk
around it after a tour inside and notice the variety of
chimneys, and the oddly shaped balconies, no two alike.
An equally imposing building is the 1902 **Old Courthouse** *(200 N. Main St. 309-827-0428. Mon.-Sat.; adm. fee),* a
domed classical revival building with exhibits on the settlement of the prairie and local history.

Kathryn Beich Inc. *(2501 Beich Rd. 309-829-1031. Mon.-
Fri. Reservations required)* has been making candy in
Bloomington since 1854. The treats are mostly machine-
made now—visitors can watch chocolate blend in copper
kettles and see how the conveyor belt operates. A glass-
covered walkway protects visitors from being splattered
with Laffy Taffy or Bit-O-Honey.

Roads in this area tend to follow the straight lines
along farm fields. The only irregularities to the flat topography are the rivers and deposits left by retreating glaciers
over 10,000 years ago. Drive south and east from Bloomington to **Moraine View State Recre-
ation Area** *(8 miles E of Downs.
309-724-8032)* to view the forested
ridges pushed up by the big ice
sheets. The park's small lake attracts
canoeists, sailors, and anglers in pur-
suit of bass and walleye. Trails and
primitive camp areas are available for
hikers and horseback riders.

The route now goes east on US
136, nearly to the Indiana border, and
south on US 136/Ill. 1 to **Danville.**
The town sits on the banks of the Vermilion River, so
named for the red clay used by Kickapoo to paint themselves. The Indians discovered the saline springs from

George Luthy Memorial Botanical Gardens

Off-Center in Peoria

Richard Nixon's White
House aide John Ehrlich-
man coined the phrase
"It'll play in Peoria"—indicating that the town was
the perfect thermometer
for taking middle Amer-
ica's temperature. But how
does the adage play in
Peoria? Some residents
read condescension in the
phrase. Peoria is not,
they say, so bland
and middle of the
road. A century ago
it was known as the
Whiskey Capital of the
World—and it has pro-
duced decidedly off-center
sons and daughters, such
as comedian Richard Pryor
and feminist Betty Friedan.

25

Field of grass, Moraine View State Recreation Area

which salt was later exported by a small Danville settlement in the 1820s. The economy is much more diversified now, including a strong recreational sector centered around the **Middle Fork Vermilion River** (*Middle Fork State Fish & Wildlife Area 217-442-4915*), Illinois's only designated national wild and scenic river. A popular river for floaters and fishermen, the Middle Fork runs through ❹ **Kickapoo State Park** (*10906 Kickapoo Park Rd. 217-442-4915*), part of a 10,900-acre preserve with nearly 20 lakes and ponds holding bass, catfish, and planted rainbow trout. In the summer, the lush green hillsides cover the scars the land suffered during the strip-mining era.

Now the route turns west on I-74, to the twin cities of **Champaign-Urbana.** Champaign is bigger and more bustling; Urbana is idyllic and more residential—the two are joined at the hip by the **University of Illinois** (*Visitor Center, Levis Faculty Center, 919 W. Illinois St. 217-333-0824*). The university has one of the finest performance facilities in the region, the **Krannert Center for the Performing Arts** (*500 S. Goodwin Ave. 217-333-6700*). Visitors pass through a marble-and-teakwood lobby to enjoy performances by nationally known artists in the concert hall, or plays in one of three theaters. The **Krannert Art Museum** (*500 E. Peabody Dr. 217-333-1860. Closed Mon.; donation*) displays an international collection of ancient and contemporary art, as well as annual shows of student and faculty works.

Northwest of Champaign-Urbana await sights that portray 19th-century life in this prairie region—the **Lake of the Woods County Park,** home to the **Early American Museum** (*1 mile N of I-74 off Ill. 47, at 600 N. Lombard St., Mahomet. 217-586-2612; June–Labor Day daily, May and Sept.-Oct. weekends; adm. fee*) and the **Mabery Gelvin Botanical Garden** (*506 N. Lombard St., Mahomet. 217-586-4389*).

Proceed southwest on Ill. 47 and I-72 to ❺ **Monticello,** a town enriched by railroads. The **Monticello Railway Museum** (*Market St. exit off I-72. 217-762-9011. May-Oct.*

Mon.-Fri.) features a collection of railroad equipment. There are also round-trip train rides *(fare)* from the museum to the **Monticello Wabash Depot** *(1 Railroad St.)*.

Two popular recreation spots along your westbound drive are **Weldon Springs State Park** *(3 miles S of Clinton off Cty. Rd. 15. 217-935-2644)*, with a small fishing lake and a restored 1865 clapboard school featuring natural history displays; and **Clinton Lake State Recreation Area** *(Cty. Rd. 14, 3 miles E of Clinton off Ill. 54. 217-935-8722)*, which allows powerboats and waterskiing on a twisting, 4,895-acre lake. The quieter areas offer good fishing for bass, bluegill, and walleye. There are boat rentals and hiking trails.

Abraham Lincoln practiced law on Illinois's Eighth Circuit, which often brought him to **Clinton,** where he sparred with political opponent Stephen A. Douglas both in the courts and on the speakers' podium (see sidebar page 23). Drive west on Ill. 10 to ❻ **Lincoln,** named in 1853 for the lawyer who drew up the town's charter. An impressive collection of the Lincoln's materials are gathered in the **Lincoln College Museum** *(McKinstry Memorial Library, 300 Keokuk St. 217-732-3155 ext. 295. Feb.–mid-Dec.)*, including his desk from the state legislature and Mary Todd Lincoln's butter knives.

Henry Ford dismantled the first Logan County Courthouse and moved it to the Henry Ford Museum and Greenfield Village in Dearborn, Michigan (see page 81), but the wooden frame **Postville Courthouse State Historic Site** *(914 5th St. 217-732-8930. Fri.-Sat.; donation)* has been

Backstage at the Krannert Center for the Performing Arts

reconstructed. Downstairs you'll find an exhibit on the traveling circuit courts—where Lincoln made the rounds—and upstairs is a re-created courtroom and county office. Just down the road stands the courthouse that succeeded Postville, the 1847 Greek Revival **Mount Pulaski Courthouse State Historic Site** *(113 S. Washington St. 217-792-3919. Tues.-Sat.)*, with artifacts from circuit court days.

Follow Ill. 54 southwest to return to Springfield.

27

Shawnee Circuit

● **400 miles** ● **2 to 4 days** ● **Year-round**

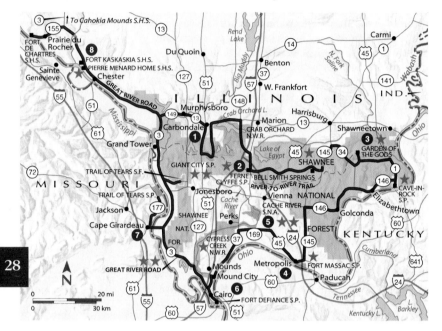

If you come from the north, you'll notice distinctive topographical changes as you make your way into southern Illinois—the country becomes hilly and thickly forested, with big broad rivers and snaky creeks everywhere. The human landscape is different, too: Accents thicken, the pace slows, and people shop at Piggly Wiggly stores. As the drive weaves in and around the Shawnee National Forest, you'll see river towns, forested hills, and cypress swamps that are more likely to remind you of the American South.

Beginning in Carbondale, the route meanders east through the Shawnee National Forest, taking in assorted state parks, a refuge, and a fort on its way to a brief stop in Paducah, Kentucky. Moving back to Illinois, the tour visits Metropolis, mythical home of Superman, and journeys along the Great River Road past the statue of another comic strip character. The drive continues north to the Trail of Tears State Forest and to Fort de Chartres near Prairie du Rocher.

The tour's starting point is ❶ **Carbondale** *(Chamber of Commerce 618-549-2146)*, which specialized in coal mining in the early 19th century. Today the city's pride is Southern Illinois University; the thickly wooded hills show few

scars from the defunct mines. The area's most striking natural wonders are protected in **Giant City State Park**★★ *(12 miles S of Carbondale, follow signs E off US 51. 618-457-4836)*, a favorite of Illinois natives. The park features relatively short walking trails and huge slabs of Makanda sandstone. Built of native rock, the park's historic lodge *(618-457-4921. Closed early Dec.–Jan.)* was constructed by the Civilian Conservation Corps in the 1930s.

Giant City State Park is part of a cluster of natural preserves that protect a big piece of the Illinois Ozarks and Shawnee Hills south of Carbondale and Marion. The **Crab Orchard National Wildlife Refuge** *(8583 Ill. 148, off Ill. 13. 618-997-3344. Day-use fee)* is home to a huge winter flock of Canada geese and nesting bald eagles. There are several boat launches along Crab Orchard Lake for anglers and sailors; bird and deer hunters also frequent the refuge. South of Crab Orchard via Ill. 148 and Ill. 37 sprawls ❷ **Ferne Clyffe State Park**★ *(Ill. 37. 618-995-2411)*, sold to the state in the 1920s by a schoolmarm who used to charge visitors

Wild Canada geese, Crab Orchard National Wildlife Refuge

ten cents. These days it's free, and you can climb wooded trails to **Hawks' Cave,** a 150-foot-long shelter cave that eroded beneath a cliff, or take the 0.5-mile **Big Rocky Hollow Trail** to an intermittent 100-foot waterfall dropping through a steep canyon. There are campgrounds and a 16-acre lake for shore fishermen, but no boating or swimming.

The parks and refuge are surrounded by **Shawnee National Forest**★ *(618-253-7114 or 800-699-6637)*, which forms an irregular belt across southern Illinois from the Mississippi River on the west to the Ohio River on the east. Illinois conservationists campaigned for a national forest in the 1920s, and the abandoned farms and eroded clear-cuts of the poverty-stricken southern hills provided the opportunity. Much of the land has now been successfully replanted, and the great swath of forest encompasses a variety of habitats, from swamps to limestone bluffs, gentle wooded hills, and sharply cut canyons. If you have sturdy boots or a good horse, and plenty of time, you can

It's a Bird, It's a Plane, It's Superman!

Tucked amid the Shawnee Hills and river towns of southern Illinois is **Metropolis,** the legendary home of Superman. Taking advantage of its name (Clark Kent worked in Metropolis, remember?), the town plays up its Superman theme to the hilt: The Chamber of Commerce even doles out kryptonite pebbles. The **Super Museum** *(517 Market St. 618-524-5518. Adm. fee)* is stuffed with more than 50,000 items of memorabilia. Visitors can see original draft comic art, Christopher Reeve's movie costume, and the original costumes of all Superman characters. One would expect that on Halloween, Superman's town would be awash with pint-size, caped defenders, right? Wrong. Reacting to the Superman saturation, the kids favor rabbits, Draculas, gorillas...anything but the Man of Steel.

take the 176-mile **River-to-River Trail** *(River-to-River Trail Society 618-252-6789),* which winds through the public lands from one side of the state to the other.

Driving east from Ferne Clyffe State Park, stop at **Bell Smith Springs** *(Forest Rd. 848)* for hikes along the caves and past the natural sandstone arch. Farther east awaits the ❸ **Garden of the Gods**★ *(Forest Rd. 114),* where a short trail leads through odd geological formations with vivid names such as Fat Man's Squeeze and Camel Rock.

Continue east to Ill. 1 and then head south to **Cave-In-Rock State Park**★ *(1 New State Park Rd. 618-289-4325),* once the redoubt of river pirates who terrorized travelers from the 55-foot-wide cave mouth. The Ohio River laps at the cave entrance, and natural light reaches into its 160-foot recesses, where visitors have unfortunately scratched messages in the sandstone. You can also camp, hike the bluffs along three different trails to the river, or eat in a stone restaurant with fine views.

If you are a quilt aficionado, plan on taking Ill. 146 to Ill. 145 and crossing the river to **Paducah, Kentucky** *(Convention & Visitors Bureau 502-443-8783 or 800-723-8224).* Located at the junction of the Tennessee and Ohio Rivers, this is the site in late April for the annual competition of the **American Quilter's Society** *(502-898-7903).* Year-round, a worthwhile stop is the **Museum of the American Quilter's Society**★ *(215 Jefferson St. 502-442-8856.*

Cave-In-Rock State Park, on the Ohio River

April-Oct. Tues.-Sun., Tues.-Sat. rest of year; adm. fee), where more than one hundred handmade quilts are on display.

Back on the Illinois side of the river, drive west on US 45 to **Fort Massac State Park**★ *(1308 E. 5th St. 618-524-4712),* a timber stockade commemorating the struggle among the French, English, and Americans for control of this key juncture along the Ohio River. Today the fort, reconstructed in 1973, sits on shady grounds along the river, with displays of 18th-century clothing and archaeological artifacts, including a huge arrowhead collection. Hike the **Hickory Nut Ridge Trail,** a nearly 3-mile scenic loop along the river east of the park. In late October, a weekend encampment features latter-day frontiersmen in period costume, as well as military bands and a voyageurs canoe race on the river.

Though ❹ **Metropolis** *(Chamber of Commerce, 610 Market St. 618-524-2714 or 800-949-5740. Mon.-Sat.)* was named long before Clark Kent became a reporter at the "Metropolis" *Daily Planet,* the town has embraced Superman as its own (see sidebar page 30), erecting a 15-foot statue of the Man of—uh—Bronze facing the business district. There's also a phone booth in the Chamber of Commerce office, where children can give the S-Man a call (but don't try changing clothes, kids). Also in town is a riverboat ***Players Casino*** *(Foot of Ferry St. 618-524-2628 or 800-929-5905),* featuring cards and one-armed bandits; cruises leave from dockside. Across from the dock rises a hotel and the **Players Theater** *(203 E. Front St. 618-524-2628. Adm. fee),* with celebrity acts, musicals, and comedy.

Museum of the American Quilter's Society, Paducah, Ky

From the river proceed northwest on US 45 and west on Ill. 169 to the bird-rich Cache River Wetlands, where 60,000 acres (and counting) have been protected by the joint efforts of private conservation groups and the ❺ **Cache River State Natural Area**★★ *(618-634-9678).* The slow-moving river looks like it got lost on its way to the Deep South, and birdwatchers, hunters, canoeists, and hikers on trails and boardwalks can join the great blue herons and bald eagles among tupelo and ancient cypress trees up to a thousand years old. Walk the 1.5-mile **Heron Pond Trail** on a floating boardwalk into the heart of the swamp. Adjacent to the natural area lies the **Cypress Creek National Wildlife Refuge**★ *(Visitor Center, Ill. 37, S of Ill. 169. 618-634-2231).*

Now drive south on Ill. 37 toward Cairo. Civil War buffs will want to stop at **Mound City National Cemetery** *(US 51 and Ill. 37),* where thousands of Union soldiers are buried next to their brothers in gray, in a shady plot that has no visitor services. It was from this southernmost tip of Illinois, at the juncture of the Ohio and Mississippi Rivers, that Gen. Ulysses S. Grant launched his campaign against the South. You'd hardly know it today when you

Cahokia Mounds

Travelers with an interest in ancient civilizations will want to make a special journey to **Cahokia Mounds State Historic Site** *(Collinsville Rd. 618-346-5160. Adm. fee)*, a 45-mile jaunt north of Prairie du Rocher, near Collinsville. As many as 30,000 people lived here from around A.D. 900 to 1200, the largest prehistoric Indian community found north of Mexico. Archaeologists have discovered artifacts indicating a complex society that grew squash and corn and built temples on great earthen mounds. The 100-foot, pyramid-shape Monks Mound is the largest of these humps, covering 14 acres. An interpretive center describes the culture of the site's original inhabitants, who mysteriously disappeared.

32

visit ❻ **Cairo** *(Chamber of Commerce 618-734-2737)*, a worn and sleepy town of ginkgo and magnolia trees, bathed in humidity. Charles Galigher, a friend of Grant's, made his fortune supplying hardtack to the Union Army. His **Magnolia Manor**★ *(2700 Washington Ave. 618-734-0201. Adm. fee)* was built in 1869 with marble fireplaces and gold-washed chandeliers. Several other fine mansions, including the bed-and-breakfast **Windham** *(2606 Washington Ave. 618-734-3247)*, line the wide, tree-shaded street.

On the narrow peninsula where the rivers meet is a raised platform from which you can observe the convergence of the blue Ohio and brown Mississippi, which merge but don't mix: Initially they form two stripes side by side in the same channel, beginning at **Fort Defiance State Park** *(US 51, E exit before bridge. 618-734-2737)*. Signs explain the crucial role of this juncture as a staging area during the Civil War.

The drive now follows portions of the **Great River Road**★★ *(Mississippi Parkway Commission 612-449-2560)*, a patchwork of highways that allows travelers to follow the Mississippi all the way from Louisiana to its source in Minnesota on both sides of the river. This is not a hurry-up route—the roads are often two-lane, and you must make time for welcome distractions that include spectacular vistas from bluffs above the river, wildlife such as bald eagles, and the sight of barges and riverboats meandering up and down the Mississippi. The twisty, island-dotted river between Cairo and Murphysboro is one of the most rewarding stretches.

Cross the river to ❼ **Cape Girardeau, Missouri** *(Convention & Visitors Bureau 573-335-1631)*, a former French trading post. The point that once jutted into the river and formed a protected cove was blasted out a century ago by the railroad. Shortly after that, a brick fire station was built that today has become the **Cape River Heritage Museum** *(538 Independence St. 573-334-0405. Wed.-Sat., or by appt.; adm. fee)*, with displays on the area's history. The town has also put much of its history in mural form, including the **Jake Wells Mural** on the campus of Southeast Missouri State University *(Kent Library, 1 University Plaza)* and the 25-panel **Missouri Wall of Fame** *(Water St. bet. Independence and Merriwether Sts.)*, located downtown along the floodwall.

Head north on Mo. 177 to the **Trail of Tears State Park** *(429 Moccasin Springs Rd. 573-334-1711. Interpretive center April-Oct. daily, Nov.-March Fri.-Sun.)*. The park is named for the harrowing journey of the exiled Cherokee tribe, who were expelled from their Southeast homeland

and sent to Oklahoma in the winter of 1838-39. An interpretive center has exhibits on the Cherokee's removal and their 800-mile march.

Return to Cape Girardeau and cross the Mississippi. Proceed north on the Illinois side of the river via Ill. 146 and Ill. 3, to the 5,114-acre **Trail of Tears State Forest** *(State Forest Rd., NW of Jonesboro. 618-833-4910)*. This Ozark forestland is the province of hikers, hunters, and horseback riders, with more than 45 miles of trails.

Continue the journey north and west along the Mississippi, stopping for at least a glance at the 6-foot statue of **Popeye the Sailor** overlooking the Mississippi in **Chester,** the birthplace of his creator, cartoonist E.C. Segar. Popeye first appeared in 1929, in a comic strip called "Thimble Theater"—a young lady named Olive Oyl took a boat trip to Africa and a spinach-eating crewman named Popeye was aboard.

Resume northwest on the Great River Road to the **Pierre Menard Home State Historic Site**★ *(4230 Kaskaskia Rd. 618-859-3031)*, a hip-roofed, French Colonial house built in 1802 by Illinois's first lieutenant governor. The house features original furnishings.

A change in the course of the Mississippi River left a chunk of Illinois, and the town of Kaskaskia, on its west bank. The old town of Kaskaskia is now underwater, but the earthworks of ❽ **Fort Kaskaskia State Historic Site** *(4372 Park Rd. 618-859-3741)* still stand atop a towering river bluff on the east bank. The fort was burned in 1766 during the French and Indian War.

Popeye the Sailor statue, Chester

33

The route continues northwest along the river to **Prairie du Rocher,** the stronghold of the French when they ruled the Mississippi Valley in the 18th century. Set on 4 acres, **Fort de Chartres State Historic Site** *(1350 Ill. 155. 618-284-7230)* has massive walls, a rebuilt chapel and guardhouse, and a museum with 18th-century artifacts. In early June and early October the fort hosts historical reenactments.

To return to Carbondale, follow the Great River Road, Ill. 149, and Ill. 13.

Ohio and Wabash

● 325 miles ● 3 to 4 days ● Year-round

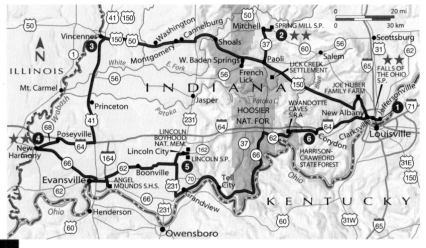

Marking Indiana's lower borders, the Ohio and Wabash Rivers have also shaped the character of southern Indiana's people and history. Settlers were drawn to the Ohio River Valley for its rich soils and the transportation potential of its waterway. The beauty of the broad Ohio River, with its limestone bluffs and forested valleys, later lured artists as well. But when railroads led to a shift of the region's commercial center north, southern Indiana sat out much of the state's industrial development. This may be the main reason it retains the rural, river-paced charm of the Old South. Its regional flavor is about as far from the Great Lakes as you can get with this guide.

This tour begins in Jeffersonville, across the Ohio River

Fossil hunting on riverbed, Falls of the Ohio State Park

from Louisville, Kentucky; it crosses west through Hoosier National Forest to the onetime frontier outpost of Vincennes, on the Wabash River, then goes south to New Harmony. After a relaxing stop in this peaceful 19th-century utopian community, the route rejoins the Ohio in thriving, much-less-peaceful Evansville. Twisting through the hilly country where Abraham Lincoln spent much of his boyhood, it arrives at Corydon, which served as the Indiana Territory's first capital, before returning to Jeffersonville.

Once a major shipbuilding town on the Ohio, ❶ **Jeffersonville** *(Chamber of Commerce 812-945-0266)* was eventually eclipsed by rival Louisville. But the town's historic connection to the river is well presented at the **Howard Steamboat Museum** *(1101 E. Market St. 812-283-3728. Closed Mon.; adm. fee)*, housed in a 22-room mansion built by Edmonds and Laura Howard in 1893. The museum contains models of Howard boats and exhibits, and a small shipyard still operates today at the old Howard site.

As a reward for fighting the British on the western frontier during the Revolutionary War, Gen. George Rogers Clark was given a large tract of land just above the Falls of the Ohio, where he founded **Clarksville** *(Chamber of Commerce 812-945-0266)*. The unnavigable falls made this a stopping point for river traffic. It's also a paleontologist's delight: The downcutting of the Ohio River has exposed a rich bed of ancient limestone fossils that runs shore to shore. **Falls of the Ohio State Park**★★ *(201 W. Riverside Dr. 812-280-9970. Closed Mon. in winter; adm. fee for interpretive center)*, with a smart new interpretive center, is surrounded by a 1,404-acre national wildlife conservation area. Coral reefs that developed here beneath a shallow sea 400 million years ago were buried and then uncovered as glaciers retreated and the river surged. When the river runs low—usually late summer and fall—visitors can walk or wade out on one of the world's largest exposed beds of Devonian fossils.

Before it became a bedroom community for Louisville, **New Albany** *(Chamber of Commerce 812-945-0266)*, reached by Ind. 62, was another robust shipbuilding town known for producing steamboats. A model of one such steamer, the 1866 *Robert E. Lee*, is displayed at the excellent **Floyd County Museum**★ *(201 E. Spring St. 812-944-7336. Tues.-Sat.; donation)*. The museum also features a collection of miniature carved dioramas of turn-of-the-century Indiana life; animated by electric motors, hundreds of characters thresh wheat and tap sugar maples.

Once Indiana's largest city, New Albany still has

Hoosiers

Only a New England Yankee might understand how it feels to be called a Hoosier—it suggests not just where you're from, but something about your character. But where did such an odd name come from? One theory is that it derives from the Saxon word *hoo*, meaning "a person of the hills"—a hillbilly. Another claims that early settlers were such no-holds-barred brawlers that they sometimes had to ask "whose ear?" at the end of an evening. More credible is a story that begins with Samuel Hoosier, an engineer who helped build the Ohio Falls Canal in the 1820s. Hoosier preferred hiring Indiana workmen to the "slackers" across the river, and his crews became known as "Hoosiers." Whatever the origin, the label today connotes proud Indiana roots, regional belonging, and, of course, a good jump shot.

35

Lost Explorers

Welsh legend tells of Madoc, a son of the Prince of Wales, who made two expeditions west to a "promising new land," but never returned from the second. Did he perish at sea or settle in the new land? In the 18th century there were reports of six skeletons found in Jeffersonville wearing Welsh armor. Then, in the 19th century, rubble discovered upriver from the falls, possibly the remains of a stone fort, rekindled the legend that Welsh explorers had arrived in the area as early as the 12th century. Even Native American stories describe fighting "white men" at the falls long before European settlers officially arrived. The mysterious skeletons are nowhere to be found, and the rubble has since been used to build local bridges, but the legend persists.

Mansion Row to show off its former glory days. The Victorian **Culbertson Mansion**★ (914 E. Main St. 812-944-9600. March-Dec. Tues.-Sun.; donation), built by a dry goods merchant in 1869, contains marble fireplaces, crystal chandeliers, and a carved rosewood staircase.

Leave New Albany on State Street, heading northwest to Scottsville Road. Ahead lies the **Joe Huber Family Farm, Orchard and Restaurant** (2421 Scottsville Rd., Starlight. 812-923-5255. March–late Dec.), where visitors pick their own produce in season or wander the fields and ponds of a farm that has been in the family since the 1840s. Another branch of the family operates the nearby **Huber Orchard and Winery** (19816 Huber Rd., Starlight. 812-923-9813. Closed Mon.), complete with petting zoo, cheese factory, and tasting room.

A drive west on US 150 brings you into **Hoosier National Forest** (812-275-5987). Here, 195,000 acres of hill country have been gradually reforested after farming eroded much of the land in the late 19th century. Hikers, mountain bikers, and horseback riders enjoy 183 miles of trails. Just south of Paoli lies the cemetery of the **Lick Creek Settlement,** where blacks fleeing slavery formed a thriving community before the Civil War.

The drive continues north of Paoli to ❷ **Spring Mill State Park**★★ (3 miles E of Mitchell, on Ind. 60. 812-849-4129. Adm. fee), a gem of a preserve with a fine mix of natural beauty and unique biology. Take a boat ride (fare) into a cave and train your flashlight on blind cave fish and crayfish. In summer, an 1814 waterpowered mill grinds cornmeal that you can buy in the park's historical village. The village includes pioneer log houses, a village store, and an apothecary shop, among other restored buildings.

Return to US 150 and head west, then turn south on Ind. 56 to **French Lick.** Best known as the hometown of basketball legend Larry Bird, the town's earlier fame stemmed from its medicinal sulfur springs—once bottled and sold as "Pluto Water"—and the resorts that developed around them. The giant brick **French Lick Springs Resort** (8670 W. Ind. 56. 812-936-9300 or 800-457-4042) retains much of its old charm, with extensive gardens, golf, and stage shows. The **Indiana Railway Museum** (Ind. 56 and Monon St. 812-936-2405. Tues. and Sat.-Sun. June-Oct., weekends April-May and Nov.; donation) has a collection of steam, diesel, and electric trains, and offers a short trolley ride (fare) or a 20-mile train journey (fare) through Hoosier National Forest. The trolley route winds northeast from French Lick to West Baden Springs, home of the 1902 **West Baden Springs Hotel**★ (Ind. 56. 317-639-4534. April-

Oct. Currently undergoing restoration), a worn architectural treasure with a domed atrium and Moorish towers.

Continuing west on US 150 toward Vincennes, you pass through Amish country, where horse-drawn plows and buggies dot the roadside. You will find Amish crafts and cuisine at **Cannelburg**'s quilt and craft show *(All Saints Cannelburg Hall)* on Labor Day weekend; and at **Gasthof** *(.75 mile N of US 50. 812-486-3977. Closed Jan.)*, a popular restaurant in **Montgomery.**

Locomotives at Indiana Railway Museum, French Lick

Proceed to ❸ **Vincennes** *(Convention & Visitors Bureau 812-886-0400 or 800-886-6443)*, on the Wabash River's east bank. The site played a crucial role in the Revolutionary War when Gen. George Rogers Clark, striving to open westward expansion, crossed the icy prairies to take the British fort here in 1779. Clark's feat is remembered at the **George Rogers Clark National Historical Park** *(401 S. 2nd St. 812-882-1776. Adm. fee)*, where a circular memorial with Greek columns contains murals depicting Clark's heroics. From 1800 to 1813, Vincennes was capital of the Indiana Territory. Here, William Henry Harrison governed an area larger than the original 13 Colonies. At Harrison's white-columned Georgian estate, **Grouseland** *(3 W. Scott St. 812-882-2096. Adm. fee)*, the President-to-be planned a campaign against Indians that resulted in the Battle of Tippecanoe...leading to his presidential campaign slogan, "Tippecanoe and Tyler Too."

The old **Indiana Territory Capitol** *(1 W. Harrison St. 812-882-7422)* is a small frame building just big enough for the nine-member general assembly that first met downstairs in 1811 and the five-member "upper house" that convened above. It's one of several historical sites managed by **Vincennes State Historic Sites** *(114 N. 2nd St. 812-882-7472. Mid-March–mid-Dec. Wed.-Sun.; donation)*.

Next follow US 41 south and I-64 and Ind. 68 west to ❹ **New Harmony**★★. The Harmonie Society, a religious group from Germany, came here to live communally in the early 1800s, but eventually moved East. The town was sold to Welsh industrialist Robert Owen, who arrived in 1824 to put his own ideas about utopia into

New Harmony, on banks of the Wabash River

practice. New Harmony became a magnet for intellectuals, and continues to attract artists and thinkers today.

Shady streets, gardens, and historical buildings make this a wonderful place to stroll. Many of the town's sites are managed by **Historic New Harmony** *(812-682-4488)*, which offers tours beginning at the **Atheneum** *(North and Arthur Sts. 812-682-4474. Fee for tours)*. Before visiting the various log cabins, Harmonist community houses, and an old opera house, pause at the Atheneum's exhibits and big-screen video for a town history primer.

Texas oil heiress Jane Blaffer Owen married a descendant of Robert Owen and pursued her own utopian vision, constructing the **New Harmony Inn**★★ *(506 North St. 812-682-4491)*, now boasting one of the Midwest's finest restaurants, the **Red Geranium** *(508 North St. 812-682-4431. Reservations suggested)*. Behind the inn sprawls

Tillich Park, featuring a dense grove of cedars where philosopher Paul Tillich is buried.

Designed by renowned architect Philip Johnson, New Harmony's **Roofless Church**★ *(Main and North Sts. 812-682-4431)* is a sculpture-dotted courtyard open to fields on the north side, with a soaring shingled dome for non-denominational services. Harmonists describe the **Labyrinth** *(Ind. 69),* a maze of hedges located eight blocks from downtown, as reflecting "the devious and difficult approach to a state of true harmony."

Resume the drive southeast on Ind. 66, to southern Indiana's largest city, **Evansville** *(Visitors Bureau 812-421-2100 or 800-433-3025).* The mid-19th-century river town is re-created in miniature, brick streets and all, in the basement of the **Evansville Museum of Arts and Sciences**★ *(411 S.E. Riverside Dr. 812-425-2406. Closed Mon.; donation).* The museum also has art exhibits and the **Koch Planetarium** *(Adm. fee).* The green silk damask walls, leaded-glass door panels, and painted ceilings at the nearby Second Empire **Reitz Home** *(224 S.E. 1st St. 812-426-1871. Mid-Jan.–Dec. Tues.-Sun.; adm. fee)* show what an 1870s lumber fortune bought. Other handsomely restored buildings include the beaux arts **Old Vanderburgh County Courthouse** *(201 N.W. 4th St.),* now housing shops; and the **Willard Library** *(21 1st Ave.).*

Docked at the riverfront, the ***City of Evansville*** *(Casino Aztar, N.W. Riverside Dr. 812-433-4400 or 800-DIAL FUN)* is a posh, vintage paddle wheeler that welcomes up to 2,700 gamblers to river cruises. East of downtown, take a peaceful walk through more than 175 acres of virgin hardwood forest, protected as part of the **Wesselman Woods Nature Preserve** *(551 N. Boeke Rd. 812-479-0771. Closed Mon.; donation).* Just outside of town at **Angel Mounds State Historic Site** *(8215 Pollack Ave. 812-853-3956. Mid-March–Dec. Tues.-Sun.; donation),* the thatched-roof dwellings of Middle Mississippian moundbuilders (A.D. 1100 to 1450) have been reconstructed.

References to Abraham Lincoln are frequent as the route moves northeast on Ind. 62, into the area where Thomas Lincoln, the President's father, settled his family in 1816, when Abe was seven years old. Facing each other across Ind. 162 near Lincoln City are the **Lincoln**

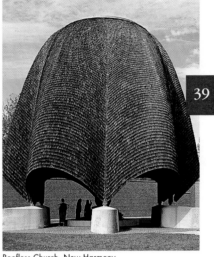
Roofless Church, New Harmony

39

Boyhood National Memorial *(US 231 and Ind. 162. 812-937-4541. Adm. fee);* and **⑤ Lincoln State Park** *(Ind. 162. 812-937-4710. Adm. fee).* The memorial's Visitor Center has Lincoln portraits and exhibits on his home and schooling.

It's a pleasant 0.5-mile hike through the woods to the rebuilt farm, and you're likely to see white-tailed deer browsing. The state park boasts four hiking trails, a swimming and boating lake, and an amphitheater where musical dramas are staged Tuesday through Sunday in summer.

The route turns south on US 231 and east on Ind. 66, along a loopy section of the Ohio River, through the Tell City Ranger District of **Hoosier National Forest** *(812-547-7051).* Trails in this area include the **Two Lakes Loop** *(Parking fee);* and the **German Ridge** and **Mogan Ridge Trails,** parts of which are open to equestrians. The **Clover Lick Barrens** provides a glimpse of a prairielike habitat, unique in this hilly region.

The limestone of southern Indiana is riddled with caves, the most famous of which is **Wyandotte Cave,** within the **Harrison-Crawford Wyandotte State Forest** *(Ind. 62, 5 miles E of Ind. 66. 812-738-2782. Closed Mon. in winter; adm. fee).* The big attraction here is

Old Vanderburgh County Courthouse, Evansville

an underground "mountain" rising 135 feet in a huge cavern room known as Rothrock Cathedral.

The drive proceeds to **⑥ Corydon,** where Indiana began in 1816; the state's first legislators wrote the state constitution beneath the "Constitution Elm" (a stump now) on High Street. In the town center stands a complex of historic structures, including the limestone **Old State Capitol Building** *(N. Capitol Ave. Closed Mon.),* which held the state senate, house, and supreme court from 1816 to 1825; and the **Governor's Headquarters** *(202 E. Walnut St. Closed Mon.),* where the state's second elected governor, William Hendricks, lived and worked. Information on these and other historic sites may be obtained from the **Corydon Historic Sites Visitors Center** *(202 E. Walnut St. 812-738-4890).*

A fine way to see the countryside is from one of the antique cars of the **Corydon Scenic Railroad** *(210 W. Walnut St. 812-738-8000. May-Oct.; fare),* which take visitors on 15-mile journeys.

Return to the Jeffersonville area via I-64.

Hoosierland★

● **340 miles** ● **3 to 4 days** ● **Year-round** ● **Peak fall foliage in Brown County appears in early to mid-Oct.**

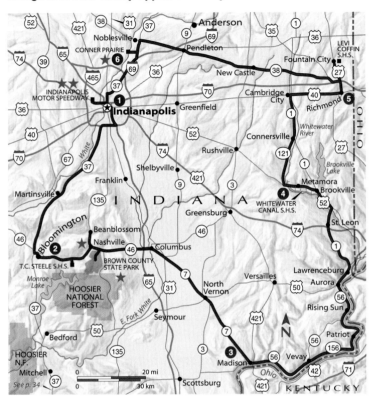

There was a time, not long ago, when some locals called Indiana's capital city "India-no-place," and counted off the days until the Indianapolis 500 in May, the one bright spot on a drab calendar. Today, though, vitality is evident year-round, spurred by a downtown rejuvenation, an explosion of spectator and participatory sports, and the livable qualities of this farm-country metropolis.

The route begins in Indianapolis and moves south to the university town of Bloomington. A state park, as well as historic and cultural sights, dot the journey east through picturesque hill country. After a stop at a 19th-century canal, the drive includes a basketball shrine, and, finally, the historic re-creations at Conner Prairie.

The streets of ❶ **Indianapolis** (*Indianapolis Convention & Visitors Association 317-639-4282*) radiate from the hub of Monument Circle, where the limestone obelisk **Soldiers' and Sailors' Monument** (*Market and Meridian Sts.*

Detail from Soldiers' and Sailors' Monument, Indianapolis

317-232-7615) stands. Within walking distance looms the domed **Indiana State Capitol** *(Capitol Ave. and Market St.)* and the **Indiana State Museum** *(202 N. Alabama St. 317-232-1637. Donation)*, with exhibits covering the age of glaciers to the present. A short walk north is the Tudor Gothic **Scottish Rite Cathedral** *(650 N. Meridian St. 317-262-3100. Tours Mon.-Fri.; donation)*, with 54 bells in its 200-foot carillon tower.

42

Indianapolis 500 race, Indianapolis Motor Speedway

Indianapolis's "new" downtown was built partly by sprucing up the old, including the 1894 **Athenaeum**★ *(401 E. Michigan St. 317-630-4569)*, inhabited now by a restaurant and theater. A big attraction drawing people back to downtown is **Circle Centre**★ *(Washington and Illinois Sts. 317-681-8000)*, a huge, modern shopping-and-entertainment complex ensconced behind the facades of historic buildings, with skywalks linking it to downtown hotels, and the **Indiana Convention Center and RCA Dome** *(Maryland St. and Capitol Ave.)*. One of those links, an eight-story glass rotunda suspended over the Washington and Illinois Streets intersection, is the **Indianapolis Artsgarden**★ ★, where you can pick up information on cultural events, cruise art exhibits, and sometimes catch a concert.

An old downtown canal is now used by paddleboaters and towpath joggers; it winds from behind the state capitol west into **White River State Park**★ *(801 W. Washington St. 317-233-2434)*, where a historic pump house serves as a Visitor Center. Within the park awaits the **Eiteljorg Museum of American Indians and Western Art**★ *(500 W. Washington St. 317-636-WEST. Mem. Day–Labor Day daily. Closed Mon. rest of year; adm. fee)*, an unusual adobe-style building with fine exhibits on various North American tribes, as well as a growing collection of Western art. Kids enjoy the park's 64-acre **Indianapolis Zoo** *(1200 W. Washington St. 317-630-2001. Adm. fee)*, with its dolphin show and train ride around the habitats of animals native to Africa and Australia.

When it comes to sports, the city is a gracious host—in addition to big-league football and basketball teams, the visiting public can use the state-of-the-art equipment and facilities at the **National Institute for Fitness and Sport** *(250 University Blvd. 317-274-3423. Fee)*.

You can't walk from downtown to the city's premier attraction, but how fitting that one must *drive* to the **Indianapolis Motor Speedway**★★ *(4790 W. 16th St. 317-484-6747. Adm. fee)*. The speedway hosts two of the biggest single-day sports events in the world: Needle-nose Indy cars chase each other around the oval at the Indianapolis 500 in May, and stock cars compete in the Brickyard 400 in August. The rest of the year, people play golf on the racetrack infield, visit the museum for a look at what the champions drove in the 1920s, and ride a tour bus *(fare)* around the track at 35 miles per hour.

Locals point with particular pride to the **Children's Museum of Indianapolis**★★ *(30th and Meridian Sts. 317-924-KIDS. Closed Mon. Labor Day–Feb.; adm. fee)*, where the buildings look like giant toys. There is plenty of noisy hands-on activity: designing miniature ships, digging for fossils, and pulling on levers at a kid-size construction site.

The **Indianapolis Museum of Art**★★ *(1200 W. 38th St. 317-923-1331. Tues.-Sun.; adm. fee)* presides over 152 acres of park and botanical gardens. Inside awaits a collection of 19th- and 20th-century European painting—including works by Monet, Renoir, Gauguin, van Gogh, and Seurat. Other treasures are the Clowes Collection of medieval and Renaissance art, and the Lilly Pavilion of Decorative Arts, housing furniture, silver, and porcelain.

You can get a feel for the Indianapolis of old by walking past the picket fences and small clapboard houses along the cobblestone streets of **Lockerbie Square**★, a German neighborhood near the downtown area. The state's best known poet, James Whitcomb Riley, resided here in the late 19th century, in what's now the **Riley Museum Home** *(528 Lockerbie St. 317-631-5885. Closed Mon. and first two weeks of Jan.; adm. fee)*. Victorian furnishings and the poet's tools—desk, pen, and paper—are on display. More upscale is the **Old Northside Historic District** *(I-65 and Pennsylvania St.)*, where you can visit the Italianate **President Benjamin Harrison Home** *(1230 N. Delaware St. 317-631-1898. Call for hours; adm. fee)*, which contains original furnishings and exhibits on the life and times of Harrison, the nation's 23rd President.

Now proceed to ❷ **Bloomington** *(Convention & Visitors Bureau 812-334-8900 or 800-800-0037)*, a university town. Trails wind through the trees of the hilly campus of **Indiana University** *(812-855-4848)*, where many buildings are made of limestone from local quarries. Murals by Thomas Hart Benton depicting the state's history adorn the walls of the **Indiana University Auditorium** *(1200 E. 7th St. 812-*

All That Jazz

Bloomington native Hoagy Carmichael began crafting witty, jazzy tunes in the 1920s and composed such hits as "Stardust," and "Heart and Soul." The **Hoagy Carmichael Room** *(Rm. 006)* in Indiana University's **Archives of Traditional Music** *(Morrison Hall. 812-855-4679. Mon.-Fri.)* documents his music career. On display are assorted memorabilia, such as his Story and Clark piano, his cornet, a 1936 Rock-ola jukebox loaded with his 78-rpm recordings, and some of his original manuscripts. The Archives of Traditional Music contain a trove of music, oral histories, and folk tales. Visitors can listen to tapes in 300 languages from the Amazon rain forest to the steppes of Asia.

43

855-9528. Mon.-Fri.), where music, theater, and dance are staged. Across the Showalter Fountain stands the **Indiana University Art Museum** ★ *(E. 7th St. 812-855-5445. Wed.-Sun.; donation).* Designed by I.M. Pei with a soaring lobby and skylight, the museum features galleries on Pre-Columbian, Byzantine, Asian, African, and modern art. Facing the fountain from the south side is the **Lilly Library** ★ *(E. 7th St. 812-855-2452. Mon.-Sat.),* with a huge collection of rare books and manuscripts ranging from a 1455 Gutenberg Bible to scripts for the *Star Trek* TV series. The **William Hammond Mathers Art Museum** *(416 N. Indiana Ave. 812-855-MUSE. Closed Mon.),* located just off campus, houses cultural artifacts—from decorated African ceramics to the broadax of an Indiana pioneer.

Continue east through hilly Brown County. The area has lured artists since the Hoosier Group discovered its fall color and quaint towns in the early 1900s. A member of this group of regional painters was Impressionist T.C. Steele, who built his House of the Singing Winds on a ridge top. Visitors can view his paintings at the **T.C. Steele State Historic Site** *(1.5 miles S of Belmont, off Ind. 46. 812-988-2785. April-Dec. Tues.-Sun.; donation),* and hike through the woods to a log cabin and nature preserve.

Once the roads were improved in this area, tourists

Books as art form, Lilly Library, Indiana University, Bloomington

followed the spoor of artists. Today weekend visitors crowd the winding streets of **Nashville** ★ *(Brown County Convention & Visitors Bureau 812-988-7303 or 800-753-3255),* frequenting numerous antique shops and galleries, including the **Brown County Art Gallery** *(Artist Dr. and E. Main St. 812-988-4609. Closed Mon.-Thurs. Jan.-Feb.),* with exhibits of local art. Nearby, an offbeat sight memorializes Indiana's infamous native son, John Dillinger, who reputedly buried much of his stolen loot around the state. At the **John Dillinger Historical Wax Museum** *(90 W. Washington St. 812-988-1933. March-Nov.; adm. fee),* you can see his handwritten notes for a bank heist, the wooden gun he used to bluff his way out of jail, and wax figures of several famous gangsters, including a gun-toting Ma Barker, and "Pretty Boy" Floyd.

Just north of Nashville, in tiny **Beanblossom,** stands the **Bill Monroe Bluegrass Hall of Fame Museum** *(On Ind. 135. 812-988-6422. Mem. Day–Oct. Tues.-Sat.; adm. fee),* founded by the late bluegrass great. Devoted to bluegrass and country music memorabilia, it's also the site of annual music festivals in June and September.

If the crowds in Nashville are too much, it's a short drive to **Brown County State Park**★ *(Ind. 135/46. 812-988-6406. Adm. fee).* You enter the park across an old covered bridge, then drive up onto the ridges for spectacular views, particularly in autumn. The park has a swimming pool, hiking and horse trails, a handsome lodge and cabins, and the Ogle Hollow Nature Preserve, with rare yellowwood trees.

Now head east on scenic Ind. 46 to **Columbus** *(Visitor Center, 506 5th St. 812-378-2622 or 800-468-6564. Closed Sun. Dec.-Feb.),* a small city with impressive architecture. Beginning in 1942 with Eliel Saarinen's sharp-edged **First Christian Church** *(531 5th St. 812-379-4491; Mon.-Fri.),* the town has erected modern buildings by the likes of I.M. Pei,

At the John Dillinger Historical Wax Museum, in Nashville

Robert Venturi, and Kevin Roche. Architectural tours *(fee)* and self-guided tour maps *(fee)* are offered at the Visitor Center.

Drop southeast on Ind. 7, to the Ohio River at ❸ **Madison** *(Convention & Visitors Bureau 812-559-2956 or 812-265-2956),* which was the state's industrial center before the Civil War. Pick up a self-guided tour brochure at **Historic Madison, Inc.** *(500 West St. 812-265-2967)* and visit the **Shrewsbury-Windle House** *(301 W. 1st St. April-Dec.; adm. fee),* the residence of a shipping magnate who installed a three-story spiral staircase. To see the medical tools of a mid-19th-century doctor, stop at **Dr. William D. Hutchings' Office** *(120 W. 3rd St. 812-265-2967. Mid-April–Oct. daily; Nov. weekends; adm. fee).* Railroad and banking bigwig J.F.D. Lanier loaned money to the state during the Civil War. The **J.F.D. Lanier State Historic Site**★ *(511 W. 1st St. 812-265-3526. Closed Mon.; donation)* features a portico overlooking the river, beautiful grounds, a garden, and dwarf fruit trees.

Just west of Madison sprawls **Clifty Falls State Park**

(*1501 Green Rd. 812-265-1331. Adm. fee March-Oct.*), where steep trails follow Clifty Creek past numerous waterfalls.

Now proceed along the Ohio through river towns settled early in the 19th century: **Vevay, Rising Sun,** and **Aurora.** Farther north awaits ❹ **Metamora,** resting on the Whitewater River. Here the state of Indiana once dreamed of a canal that would spur commerce between the Ohio River and the National Road. Building the canal bankrupted the state in the 1840s, but it once again owns a 14-mile section of the waterway. Visitors can board a horse-drawn canalboat, the ***Ben Franklin III*** (*May-Oct.; fare*), or visit a waterpowered gristmill at the **Whitewater Canal State Historic Site** (*US 52. 765-647-6512. Mid-March–mid-Dec. Tues.-Sun., boat runs May-Oct.*).

Go north to US 40, formerly called the National Road (see sidebar page 64), and turn east. In industrial ❺ **Richmond** you'll find a stretch of highway known as Antique Alley. The **Wayne County Historical Museum** (*1150 North A St. 765-962-5756. Feb.-Dec. Tues.-Sun., and by appt.; adm. fee*) has a motley collection of pioneer artifacts, industrial products, and, of all things, an Egyptian mummy.

The Underground Railroad (see sidebar page 83) ferrying slaves to freedom also passed this way. The **Levi Coffin State Historic Site** (*113 N. Main St., Fountain City. 765-847-2432. June-Aug. Tues.-Sat., Sept.-Oct. Sat.; adm. fee*) honors the work of a couple who assisted in this effort. On view are a restored house with Quaker furnishings, artifacts of escaped slaves, and vintage buggies.

46

Memorabilia, Indiana Basketball Hall of Fame, New Castle

Turn west on Ind. 38. A stop in **New Castle** will confirm that the movie *Hoosiers* was no fiction: At the **Indiana Basketball Hall of Fame** (*1 Hall of Fame Court. 765-529-1891. Closed Mon.; adm. fee*), high school letter jackets and uniforms of hoopsters such as Oscar Robertson and Larry Bird are treated like holy relics.

Next stop near Noblesville, at ❻ **Conner Prairie**★ (*13400 Allisonville Rd. 317-773-0666 or 800-966-1836. Museum open year-round, grounds April-Nov. Tues.-Sun.; adm. fee*), former home of fur trader William Conner. Here visitors can try such 19th-century chores as soapmaking and logsplitting. The site features a museum, historical buildings, costumed guides, and lectures and reenactments.

To return to Indianapolis, take I-69 and Ind. 37.

Lakeshore and Farms

● **265 miles** ● **2 to 3 days** ● **Year-round** ● **Beware of autumn ice storms caused by the "lake effect."**

Few regions of the country embody such contrasts as northern Indiana, from the rust belt smokestacks of cities near Portage to the peaceful fields of Amish farmers, where autos from the nearby assembly lines are stoically rejected. Once the area was mostly marshland and prairie, left behind by retreating glaciers, but a century of reclamation has changed that; now, the last parcels of bogs and fens are considered rare and valuable habitat.

This route begins in the town that Studebaker built, South Bend, then moves on to the migrating sand dunes along Lake Michigan, and through the cornfields of Indiana's interior. After a visit to Fort Wayne, it heads north into the swampy woods around the Pigeon River, a haven for nesting birds that contrasts sharply with the hive of industry not far away. It returns to South Bend through picturesque Amish country.

For a city that has manufactured everything from sports cars to sewing machines, ❶ **South Bend**★ *(Chamber of Commerce 219-234-0051)* is nevertheless something of a garden spot, with some elegantly landscaped mansions and the beautiful campus of the **University of Notre Dame** *(Notre Dame Ave. and Dorr Rd. 219-631-5000. Tour reservations required)*. Visitors to Notre Dame can take a guided walking tour or make their own way to the **Grotto of Our Lady of Lourdes** (a faithful copy of the original miracle site in France) and the Gothic **Basilica of the Sacred Heart**.

A blacksmith shop owned by Henry and Clement Studebaker supplied the Union Army with wagons during

Basilica of the Sacred Heart, University of Notre Dame

Lakeshore and Farms

Dune Ecology

The concept of ecology is commonplace now, but when botanist Henry Cowles began studying the Indiana Dunes around the turn of the century, few scientists had systematically studied the way species in evolving habitats interact and sustain one another. Cowles, who taught at the University of Chicago, was fascinated by the enormous variety of plant species at Indiana Dunes: over 1,400, ranging from glacier plants such as bearberry to desert inhabitants such as prickly pear cactus. It was here that he conducted groundbreaking studies of plant succession. He documented, for instance, how marram grass anchors a dune and then paves the way for other plants to grow in its decomposing humus. Thanks to Cowles, the Indiana Dunes are known as the birthplace of modern ecology.

the Civil War—by the 1930s, their company was one of the nation's premier car producers. The **Studebaker National Museum** ★ *(525 S. Main St. 219-235-9714. Adm. fee)* shows off the products of the now defunct company, from a Conestoga wagon to a tall-finned Packard Predictor.

The ghost of Notre Dame football legend Knute Rockne no doubt visits the **College Football Hall of Fame** *(111 S. St. Joseph St. 219-235-9999. Adm. fee)*, where college banners fly above the stadiumlike entrance. You can test your pigskin skills on the Practice Field, or get a 360-degree video view of the action in a big game.

The **Northern Indiana Center for History** *(808 W. Washington St. 219-235-9664. Closed Mon.; adm. fee)* sits in a neighborhood of beautiful 19th-century mansions. Displays describe the plight of fugitive slaves, as well as the goods made in South Bend's younger days. The center provides tours of nearby **Copshaholm** ★ ★ *(Mid-Feb.– mid-Jan.)*, a huge 1896 mansion with a plaster frieze of musicians encircling its music room, among other lavish details. Also on the grounds, and offering quite a contrast, stands the **Dom Robotnika,** typical of the dwellings inhabited by factory workers in the 1930s.

South Bend is one of the few cities in America that can offer a white-water kayaking run through its downtown area. The **East Race Waterway** ★ *(126 N. Niles Ave. 219-235-9401. June-Aug.; fee)* is a 2,000-foot-long artificial channel diverted from the St. Joseph River. The flow is regulated to provide frothy waves for international competitors or placid paddling for families; equipment can be rented at the waterway.

The route goes west on Ind. 2 and US 20 to the Lake Michigan shore and ❷ **Michigan City** *(Visitors Bureau 219-872-5055),* once, believe it or not, a busier port than Chicago. Those days are long gone, though this small city remains a popular launching point for sportfishing. A 1904 lighthouse still operates on the east pier. An even earlier beacon, erected in 1858, is now the **Old Lighthouse Museum** *(Heisman Harbor Rd. 219-872-6133. Closed Mon.; adm. fee)*, with a giant, restored Fresnel lens and exhibits of Great Lakes maritime lore.

West on US 12, sand dunes ribbon the coast of Lake Michigan in one of the world's most intriguing ecosystems. The undulating dunes offer an extraordinary diversity of habitat, from swamps to massive sand canyon "blowouts" where vegetation has surrendered its rooty grip to the wind off the lake. **Indiana Dunes National Lakeshore** ★ ★ encloses 13,000 acres of beach, bogs, and

woods. Exhibits on the ecology and history of the dunes are found outdoors, at the **Visitor Center** *(US 12 and Kemil Rd. 219-926-7561. Adm. fee),* and at the 1822 **Joseph Bailly Homestead** and adjacent **Chellberg Farm** *(Mineral Springs Rd., off US 12. Grounds open daily, building tours Sun. Mem. Day–Oct.).* Take some time to hike between sandhills to the uncrowded beach.

Surrounded by the lake-shore, **Indiana Dunes State Park**★★ *(Ind. 49. 219-926-1952. Adm. fee)* offers an extensive trail system through its 2,182 acres of marshes, sculptured dunes, and sand "mountains" that are on the move at the rate of a yard or so a year. There is also a swimming beach and a pavilion, and a nature center with exhibits on dune ecology. For a sunset, climb to the top of 192-foot **Mount Tom.**

Farther west along Lake Michigan, the industrial stacks begin to rise like asparagus stalks, but at **Portage** *(Chamber of Commerce 219-762-3300)* you still can choose sportfishing over steel foundries. Arrange a charter at one of the areas many marinas—try Portage Public Marina *(219-763-6833)*—to fish the rejuvenated lake for salmon and trout from April to November.

Indiana Dunes National Lakeshore on Lake Michigan

The route turns inland now along I-65 and US 30, through cultivated cornfields and small towns. The **Farmers' Market** *(Porter County Courthouse lawn, 16 E. Lincolnway. June-Oct. Tues. and Thurs.)* in **Valparaiso** *(Chamber of Commerce 219-462-1105)* is a real treat, this being the hometown of popcorn icon Orville Redenbacher. The town celebrates that explosive crop with a festival every fall.

Continue on US 30 to **Plymouth** *(Chamber of Commerce 219-936-9000 or 800-626-5353),* where much of the swampy land has been transformed to farms. There's enough damp ground to grow a good blueberry crop, though, and every Labor Day weekend the county holds a three-day blueberry festival. Southwest of town in the Twin Lakes area stands a life-size statue of **Chief Menominee** *(S. Peach Rd., S of W. 12th Rd.)*. The Potawatomi leader held out against the government until 1838, when his band was forced on a "Trail of Death" to Kansas.

Corn harvest, Twin Lakes area

If farm after farm seems monotonous to you, stop at little ❸ **Mentone** *(Chamber of Commerce 219-353-7417),* "the egg basket of the Midwest," and visit the 11-foot-tall, 3,000-pound concrete egg erected on Main Street. The farms in this area produce just about everything: eggs, corn, soybeans, potatoes, pumpkins, and milk. City slickers can get some help with a self-guided agricultural tour at the **Kosciusko County Convention & Visitors Bureau** *(313 S. Buffalo St. 219-269-6090).*

Proceed east on Ind. 25 and US 30 to the robust city of ❹ **Fort Wayne** *(Visitors Bureau, 1021 S. Calhoun St. 219-424-3700 or 800-767-7752),* a crossroads into which rivers flow north and south. The area has been occupied by Indians, fur traders, and British troops, a legacy that is recounted at the **Old City Hall Historical Museum** *(302 E. Berry St. 219-426-2882. Feb.-Dec. Tues.-Sun.; adm. fee).* Here you can spend a few minutes behind the bars of an 1890s jail, plus examine exhibits ranging from antebellum ladies' dresses to vintage tools and toys. History buffs will also appreciate the extensive collection of Abraham Lincoln photographs and memorabilia at the **Lincoln Museum**★ *(200 E. Berry St. 219-455-3864. Closed Mon.; adm. fee).* The museum reconstructs rooms from different periods in Lincoln's life, and has interactive educational exhibits.

Though Fort Wayne today is a manufacturing and trade center, it is also the resting place of John Chapman—aka Johnny Appleseed, the tree-planting legend. His grave is surrounded by **Johnny Appleseed Memorial Park** *(Behind Memorial Coliseum, on Parnell Ave. 219-427-6003),* a shady 43-acre green space bisected by the St. Marys River.

A short drive north from Fort Wayne lies **Auburn,** a little farm town that was once home to the Auburn Automobile Company. Led by Errett "E.L." Cord, the company produced stylish Cords and Duesenbergs, including the

luxurious Duesenberg Model J, the ultimate snob car of the 1930s. The original factory showroom that is now the **Auburn Cord Duesenberg Museum**★ *(1600 S. Wayne St. 219-925-1444. Adm. fee)* displays classic cars from early steam and electrics to more recent racers.

Zigzag north to **Rome City,** where the novelist and photographer Gene Stratton-Porter built a house by Sylvan Lake named Limberlost North. Almost a century ago, Porter's best-selling novel, *The Girl of the Limberlost,* painted a romantic picture of life in the Indiana swamps—even as farmers were draining the bug-infested wetlands as quickly as they could. The **Gene Stratton-Porter State Historic Site** *(1205 Pleasant Point. 219-854-3790. Mid-March–mid-Dec. Tues.-Sun.; donation)* preserves the author's 16-room "cabin" and beloved wildflower gardens.

Now go farther north for a look at the marshes and wetlands that were once characteristic of northern Indiana. The **❺ Pigeon River State Fish and Wildlife Area**★ *(8310 E. Cty. Rd. 300N, Mongo. 219-367-2164. Daily in winter, Mon.-Fri. in summer)* protects 12 miles along the Pigeon River and offers camping, hunting, and fine fishing. Birdwatchers look for herons, Carolina wrens, and wild turkeys, and visitors can pick berries and mushrooms.

Classic cars, Auburn Cord Duesenberg Museum

51

Continue on to **Elkhart County** *(Convention & Visitors Bureau 219-262-8161 or 800-860-5957),* into the land of the Amish. Many of the farms that replaced the area's swamps are now plowed by Amish families—without the aid of newfangled machinery. The Amish-Mennonite story, from their beginnings in Switzerland to their plain lifestyle, is told in **Shipshewana** at **Menno-Hof**★ *(510 S. Van Buren St. 219-768-4117. Jan.-March Tues.-Sat., Mon.-Sat. rest of year; donation).* Though the Amish eschew modern lifestyles, there are plenty of entrepreneurs here selling fabrics, crafts, and foods. Numerous area restaurants offer Amish fare—try the **Blue Gate Restaurant** *(Ind. 5 and Middlebury St., Shipshewana. 219-768-4725. Mon.-Sat.),* located in the **Riegsecker Marketplace** *(195 N. Van Buren St.),* full of little shops that sell Amish handcrafted furniture and household items; or the **Village Inn Restaurant** *(107 S. Main St. 219-825-2043. Mon.-Sat.)* in Middlebury.

Follow US 20 back to South Bend.

● 345 miles ● 2 to 3 days ● Year-round

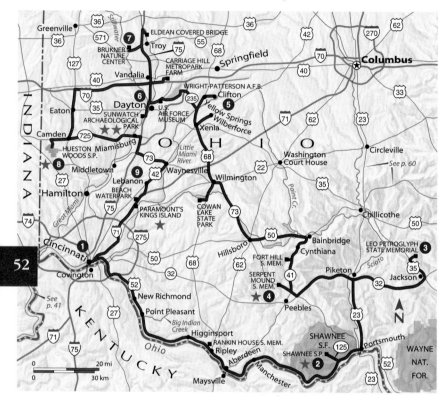

While northern Ohio prospered from the commercial might of the Great Lakes, the southern part of the state focused in another direction, looking south for trade and raw materials that could be ferried along its rivers. Wiggling along the state's southern boundary, the Ohio River flows from the Appalachian Plateau, where the hills and steep hollows sustain thick forests with brilliant fall colors. As the river deepens and broadens going west, the towns get bigger and more cosmopolitan—none more so than Cincinnati, a busy and diverse river city, with plenty of pride and hard work under its belt.

After beginning with the rich cultural offerings of Cincinnati, this drive turns southeast along the winding, languorous path of the Ohio River, visiting historic houses and Appalachian hill country. It then moves north, passing intriguing prehistoric sights on its way to Dayton, another city that thrived as a trade center. The route strays north of Dayton for another dose of natural beauty before

zigzagging south to varied historic sights, and concluding with amusement parks on Cincinnati's northeast edge.

In the early 19th century, **❶ Cincinnati** *(Convention & Visitors Bureau 513-621-2142 or 800-621-7805)* was the biggest city in what was considered the "Far West." You are reminded of that era on entering the soaring temple-like arch framing the doorway to the **Cincinnati Museum Center**★★ *(1301 Western Ave. 513-287-7000 or 800-733-2077. Adm. fee for museums and theater)*. Built as a railroad terminal in 1933, the center has an art deco lobby ringed with historical murals. Ramps on either side lead not to trains (only a small Amtrak service remains here), but to museums: the **Cincinnati History Museum**★ on one side, with a frontier river-town street and an exhibit on World War II; and the marvelous, kid-oriented **Museum of Natural History & Science**★, which takes you underground in a re-created limestone cavern, and makes ice age geology the stuff of a detective story.

Old Cincinnati nestled in a basin by the Ohio River; as it prospered, wealthier folk moved up the hills, where the city's fine parks were built. One of these, **Eden Park**★

(Eden Park Dr., off Gilbert Ave. 513-352-4080) offers grand views of the river and city. Within it stands the excellent **Cincinnati Art Museum**★ *(953 Eden Park Dr. 513-721-5204. Closed Mon.; adm. fee)*, with art collected from around the

Cincinnati after dark

world and some local originals, such as handpainted Rookwood pottery. Also located in the park are the **Krohn Conservatory** *(1501 Eden Park Dr. 513-421-4086)*, housing 5,000 species of rare and exotic plants, with a fragrant rain forest in its center; and the **Cincinnati Playhouse in the Park** *(962 Mount Adams Circle. 513-421-3888. Call for performance schedule; adm. fee)*, a hilltop theater that began as a drama student project in 1960 and grew to mount stages productions with stars such as Lynn Redgrave.

Cincinnati was the birthplace of William Howard Taft, one of seven Presidents born in Ohio. The son of a diplomat, Taft's boyhood home is now the **William Howard Taft National Historic Site** *(2038 Auburn Ave. 513-684-3262),* a Greek Revival structure containing exhibits on his life and legacy. His half brother, Charles Phelps Taft, amassed a substantial art collection early in this century that includes works by Rembrandt, Gainsborough, and Turner. His luxurious home is now the **Taft Museum**★ *(316 Pike St. 513-241-0343. Adm. fee),* where you should keep an eye peeled for the recently restored murals (in the front hall) painted by African-American artist Robert S. Duncanson.

For a little sunshine and sport, visit **Cinergy Field** *(201 E. Pete Rose Way. 513-352-5400. Call for schedule; adm. fee),* which will remind you that in 1869, long before Pete Rose and Johnny Bench played ball, the Cincinnati Red Stockings became the country's first fully professional baseball team.

The route leaves Cincinnati and heads southeast on uncrowded US 52, along the Ohio River. Near Big Indian Creek, in the shady little town of **Point Pleasant,** stands

Rankin House State Memorial above the Ohio River

the **Ulysses S. Grant Birthplace** *(Jct. of US 52 and Ohio 232. 513-553-4911 or 800-796-4282. April-Oct. Wed.-Sun.; donation),* a small white clapboard home with furnishings that roughly date from 1822, when the future Civil War general and President was born.

A short ride farther on US 52 leads to a small brick house perched high above the river, a key stop on the Underground Railroad that helped transport escaped slaves to the North (see sidebar page 83). The **Rankin House State Memorial** *(Rankin Rd. 937-392-1627. Wed.-Sun. Mem. Day–Labor Day, weekends late April–Mem. Day and Labor Day–Oct.; adm. fee)* preserves the home of Rev. John Rankin, whose lighted windows were the goal of slaves crossing the river, and whose stories helped inspire Cincinnati resident Harriet Beecher Stowe as she wrote *Uncle Tom's Cabin.*

Continue on US 52 through an area nicknamed "Little Smokies" for its hazy hills carved by deep ravines and splashed with redbud and dogwood blossoms in spring.

A prize piece of forest is preserved in **❷ Shawnee State Park**★ *(Ohio 125. 614-858-6652. Adm. fee)* and in the surrounding 60,000-acre **Shawnee State Forest.** Some of the deeper hollows have never been cut for lumber, but in any case thick forest, dominated by oak and hickory, has

Bird's-eye view of Serpent Mound

grown everywhere. There are hiking trails and two-track roads, two lakes, the Ohio River, a 5,000-acre wilderness area, and the attractive **Shawnee Resort** *(614-858-6621)*.

The pleasures of living by a river are sometimes offset by the dangers—a big flood can carry everything away. Most river towns build floodwalls, but nearby **Portsmouth** went a step further. Artist Robert Dafford painted a quarter mile of murals on the **Portsmouth Floodwall** *(Front St.)*, which depicts the town in its heyday, around the century's turn. Local history and regional art are also featured in town at the **Southern Ohio Museum** *(825 Gallia St. 614-354-5629. Closed Mon.; adm. fee)*, where music and theater performances are staged.

Though there are many unanswered questions about the ancient peoples who lived in the Ohio Valley, there are hints of sophisticated and spiritual cultures. To observe some interesting petroglyphs, head north on US 23, east on Ohio 32, and north on US 35 to the **❸ Leo Petroglyph State Memorial** *(Cty. Rd. 59. 614-286-2487)*, which consists of 37 images—including bird figures, feet, and a human head—carved into a slab of sandstone more than seven centuries ago. Nature trails offer hiking opportunities through the hills around the petroglyphs.

For another prehistoric mystery, backtrack west on Ohio 32, picking up Ohio 73 northwest. If you saw the **❹ Serpent Mound State Memorial**★ *(Ohio 73, near Peebles. 937-587-2796. Daily Mem. Day–Labor Day, weekends*

April–Mem. Day and Labor Day–Oct.; adm. fee) from the sky, it would resemble a squiggly snake, with what appears to be an egg in its mouth. At the memorial you can climb an observation tower, walk around and over the mound—it's over 1,300 feet long and 20 feet wide—and visit the museum, which displays artifacts dug up around the site.

Now head north on Ohio 41 to **Fort Hill State Memorial** *(13614 Fort Hill Rd., near Cynthiana. 937-588-3221)*, a hilltop fortification believed to be the work of Hopewell Indians some 1,500 to 2,000 years ago. Nature trails wind throughout the 1,200-acre site, and you may hear warblers singing as you search for rare flowers such as moss phlox.

At the U.S. Air Force Museum

Heading northwest, the route moves off the Appalachian Plateau and into a gentler topography smoothed by retreating glaciers 12,000 years ago. Ancient fossil beds have been uncovered along Cowan Creek where it flows in and out of the man-made lake at **Cowan Lake State Park** *(729 Beechwood Rd. 513-289-2105. Adm. fee)*, south of Wilmington via US 68. There are marinas on the lake for sailboats and small powerboats, and anglers pursue smallmouth bass, crappie, and walleye.

For a look at one of the country's largest museums devoted to African-American culture, take US 68 north and US 42 northeast to Wilberforce and the **National Afro-American Museum and Cultural Center** ★ *(1350 Brush Row Rd. 513-376-4944. Closed Mon.; adm. fee)*. Rotating exhibits focus on different themes, including music traditions, landscapes, heritage, and crafts.

The dolomite left in this region by ancient ocean sediments has been cut by streams into steep gorges. One of the most spectacular can be found in ❺ **Clifton.** The **Clifton Gorge State Nature Preserve** ★ *(Ohio 343. 937-964-8794)* surrounds a 70-foot drop of the Little Miami River, where pockets in the steep walls nurture wildflowers and some rare white cedars, and thick forests put on a fall color show. Nearby stands **Clifton Mill** *(75 Water St. 937-767-5501. Wed. and Fri.-Mon.; adm. fee)*, which harnesses the river to power a gristmill. Tours show how the grinding process turns grain into pancake mix and cornmeal.

When it comes to promoting itself, Dayton often emphasizes aviation. It's entitled—Wilbur and Orville Wright first tinkered with flying machines in their Dayton bike shop, and today the Wright-Patterson Air Force Base hugs the city's eastern side. As you head toward Dayton, northwest on Ohio 235 and southwest on Ohio 444, stop at the **U.S. Air Force Museum**★★ *(Wright Field, Springfield Pike. 513-255-3286)*, a place so huge you might want to taxi around its hangars in a little XF-85 "Goblin" rather than walk. From Orville Wright's original wind tunnel to the F-117 Stealth fighter, there is little missing from the evolutionary chain of aircraft and aviation artifacts here. When your legs get tired you can prop them up in the cockpit of a fighter plane. A shuttle runs to a hangar that holds several retired presidential aircraft.

National Afro-American Museum and Cultural Center

Now head on to

❻ **Dayton** *(Convention & Visitors Bureau 937-226-8211 or 800-221-8234)*, built on the banks of the Great Miami River to take advantage of fertile ground and the river's commercial opportunities. Although flooding was a constant threat, the city became a hive of industry, producing everything from cash registers to starter motors. A carefully designed flood management plan has finally controlled all but the worst flooding.

Sites tying the city to aviation are linked by an **Aviation Trail**★; brochures describing the sights on these routes are available from Aviation Trail, Inc. *(P.O. Box 633, Dayton, 45409. 937-443-0793)*, or at the redbrick **Wright Cycle Company Shop** *(22 S. Williams St. 937-225-7705. Mem. Day–Labor Day daily, Labor Day–Mem. Day weekends)*, which is naturally on the route. This is where the brothers ran a bicycle shop and printing business from 1897 to 1896. You can see the 1905 *Flyer III*—their first "practical" plane, according to Orville, at the **Carillon Historical Park**★ *(2001 S. Patterson Blvd. 937-293-2841. May-Oct. Tues.-Sun.; adm. fee)*. This pleasant spot, situated outside a deep curve in the Great Miami River, is home to the 1796 Newcom Tavern (Dayton's oldest standing building), an old covered

57

bridge, and a number of classic railroad cars and engines.

There are other gems in Dayton that sometimes get overlooked: the handsome **Old Court House Museum** (*7 N. Main St. 937-228-6271. Tues.-Sat.*), an 1850 Greek Revival building with exhibits on the Wright brothers and the Miami Valley; and the **Paul Laurence Dunbar House State Memorial** (*219 N. Paul Laurence Dunbar St. 937-224-7061. Mem. Day–Labor Day Wed.-Sat., Sept.-Oct. weekends; adm. fee*), the home of the black poet who published 21 books and spoke out for justice for African Americans at the turn of the century.

SunWatch Archaeological Park★★ (*2301 W. River Rd. 937-268-8199. Closed Mon. Nov.-March; adm. fee*) is virtually hidden in the industrial clutter of Dayton's outskirts. Archaeologists have uncovered the remains of a farming community that lived here on the riverbanks in the late 12th century, and they've done a masterful job of reconstruction. The site gives a clear snapshot of a matrilineal society with upper- and lower-class neighborhoods.

Heading north of Dayton on I-75, jog briefly east on I-70 and north on Ohio 201 to the **Carriage Hill MetroPark Farm** (*7800 E. Shull Rd. 937-879-0461*), centered around the historical working farm of a late 19th-century German settler. Interpreters man the forge at the blacksmith shop and run the country store, icehouse, and summer kitchen. Continue north on I-75 to Troy, and go west on Ohio 55 to the **7 Brukner Nature Center** (*5995 Horseshoe Bend Rd. 937-698-6493. Fee on Sun. only*), a wildlife refuge with 6 miles of hiking trails through 165 acres of forest, swamp, prairie, and along the Stillwater River. The preserve has a condensed feel, and the exhibits are simple (some handwritten), but informative. On Troy's other side stands one of Ohio's longest covered bridges, the 1860 **Eldean Covered Bridge** (*2 miles N of Troy on Cty. Rd. 25A*). Cars can still drive across the span.

Return south on I-75 and head west on I-70, south on US 127, and west on Ohio 725 to **8 Hueston Woods State Park**★ (*Ohio 732. 513-523-6347*), a rare patch of virgin Ohio forest that was allowed to stand (probably because its maples were valued for syrup) while farms were cleared two centuries ago. Beech-maple forest once covered most of Ohio, but now it's a rarity and a wonderful place to hike and relax. Pileated woodpeckers, uncommon in Ohio, also survive here. The park has a lake, fossil beds, and a big lodge (*513-423-6381 or 800-282-7275*) with meals and accommodations.

Presidential Legacies

Ohio can name seven U.S. Presidents as native sons, an impressive boast until you look at which Presidents we're talking about. Ulysses S. Grant, Rutherford B. Hayes, James A. Garfield, Benjamin Harrison, William McKinley, William Howard Taft, Warren G. Harding...no one is unpacking the chisels at Mount Rushmore for that pantheon. Even Grant was a better general than he was a President. At the Greek-columned museum at Hayes's Spiegel Grove, an elderly woman contemplated the grave of the nation's 19th President and asked, "Didn't he get impeached or something?" (No—but he lost the popular election to Democrat William Tilden, and won the job in the Electoral College.) It's been awhile since Ohio fielded a presidential candidate and if the Buckeyes aren't careful, some other state will catch up. Where is the next William Howard Taft, or Warren G. Harding?

58

Just east on Ohio 725 you'll reach **Miamisburg** and the **Miamisburg Mound** *(Mound Ave. 937-866-4532)*, a 65-foot mound of earth amassed by the Adena as long as 3,000 years ago. Within it are two burial chambers; atop it (there are stairs) awaits an excellent view of the Miami Valley.

Zigzag south to ❾ **Lebanon** via I-75, Ohio 73, and US 42 to the **Golden Lamb Inn**★ *(27 S. Broadway. 513-*

Eldean Covered Bridge, Troy

932-5065), where you can follow the footsteps of Mark Twain and Charles Dickens. Serving meals since 1803, this old stagecoach stop is outfitted with furniture made by a Shaker community that once dwelled nearby. Check out Lebanon's antique shops or take a sight-seeing excursion ride on the **Turtle Creek Valley Railway** *(198 S. Broadway. 513-398-8584. May-Oct. Wed. and Fri.-Sun., April and Nov. Sat.-Sun.; fare)*. Most of the cars date from the 1930s, and there is an open car for good weather.

Now pick up I-71 south to cap the drive with a visit to some family-oriented theme parks. The first is the popular **Beach Waterpark** *(2590 Waterpark Dr., Mason. 513-398-SWIM or 800-886-SWIM. Mem. Day–Labor Day; adm. fee)*. Farther down spawls its competitor, **Paramount's Kings Island**★ *(6300 Kings Island Dr., Mason. 513-573-5800. Mem. Day–late Aug. daily, April and Oct. selected weekends; adm. fee)*, featuring twisting roller coasters and rides inspired by movies.

Return to Cincinnati via I-71 south.

● **540 miles** ● **3 to 4 days** ● **Year-round**

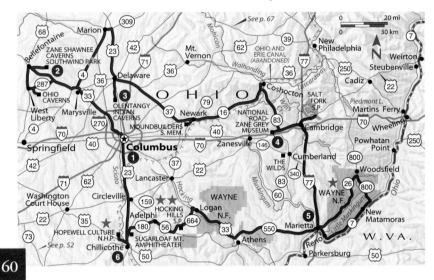

To occupy the middle of Ohio is to occupy the middle of the middle: where west meets east, north abuts south, mountains border plains, and the various immigrant races that settled America blend. A cross section of central Ohio is a portrait of typical America…but of course there is no such thing. Perhaps, though, this is the best we can do: a region where the landscape varies from flat farm country to steep Appalachian hollows, where the highway of history is shared by Indian trails, mule-drawn canalboats, and the asphalt National Road, and where the ground has been occupied by vastly different cultures dating back to the mysterious, ancient Mound Builders.

This journey begins in the state capital, Columbus, and after visiting some sites in the farm country and towns just to the north, it heads east and up onto the Allegheny Plateau. After pausing at historic Marietta and taking a scenic drive through Wayne National Forest, the route twists up gorges and over ridges in the exquisite Hocking Hills. The topography begins to smooth again at Chillicothe, and then it's back to Columbus.

❶ **Columbus** *(Convention & Visitors Bureau 614-221-CITY or 800-345-4FUN)* was not much more than swampland before it was chosen to be the state capital in 1812, so the city grew up around the **Ohio Statehouse** *(High and Broad Sts. 614-728-2695 or 888-OHIO123)*, a Doric-columned Greek Revival building with a flat-topped cupola.

Batelle Riverfront Park, along the Scioto River near

downtown, is a peaceful place to walk. Moored here is a full-scale duplicate of the **Santa Maria** *(Marconi Blvd. and W. Broad St. 614-645-8760. Sat.-Sun. April–Mem. Day and Labor Day–Oct., Wed.-Sun. Mem. Day–Labor Day; adm. fee),* one of the ships Christopher Columbus sailed to the New World; you can see what a cramped journey it was if you tour the 98-foot ship.

Columbus has some neighborhoods of distinctive character: the entertainment-oriented **Brewery District** *(Roughly bounded by S. Front, Whittier, and S. High Sts. and Livingston Ave.);* and particularly the nearby **German Village**★, a 19th-century working-class neighborhood that has become a yuppie enclave of coffee shops and art galleries. A special commission ensures historic verisimilitude of the architecture along its brick streets and tree-lined sidewalks. The **German Village Society Meeting Haus** *(588 S. 3rd St. 614-221-8888)* has maps and tour information, but you can enjoy walking around on your own. Pick up a guidebook at the the rambling **Book Loft** *(631 S. 3rd St. 614-464-1774)* and squeeze through 32 cramped rooms of discounted books.

Columbus Brewing Co. in the Brewery District

Columbus discovered America, but America discovered Columbus through the writings of James Thurber, who once wrote, "The clocks that strike in my dreams are often the clocks of Columbus." The **Thurber House**★ *(77 Jefferson Ave. 614-464-1032),* where the *New Yorker* writer and managing editor lived with his family during his college years, is lovingly kept as it was in 1913-17. The Thurber Center next door offers readings and seminars, a bookstore, and many of Thurber's whimsical drawings.

Heading north out of downtown, stop by another vibrant neighborhood, the **Short North** *(N. High St. bet. Nationwide Blvd. and 5th Ave.),* filled with galleries and a public market *(59 Spruce St.).* Then for a good grasp of Ohio history, natural history, and prehistoric Indian cultures, spend some time studying the exhibits at the **Ohio Historical Center and Ohio Village**★ *(I-71 and 17th Ave. 614-297-2300 or 800-OLD-OHIO. Center open year-round, village open April-Nov. Wed.-Sun., Feb.-March weekends; adm. fee).* The

61

village re-creates a typical Ohio county seat from the Civil War era, with everything from a Masonic Lodge to a tin shop, staffed by costumed interpreters. Old-style meals are served at the Colonel Crawford Inn.

Finally, for those with a bent for beer, domestic genre, tour the **Anheuser-Busch Brewery** *(700 Schrock Rd. 614-847-6465. Mon.-Sat.),* in which you walk, alone or with a guide, down corridors lined with history displays and

windows with views of the working brewery. During Prohibition, the company survived by selling ice cream and malt syrup, among other things. There is, of course, a hospitality room at the end of the tour.

The route leaves Columbus now, traveling northwest into some of Ohio's best cave country. Here, limestone has been eaten away by underground water to create interesting formations such as caverns at ❷ **Zane Shawnee Caverns Southwind Park** *(7092 State Rte. 540, Bellefontaine. 937-592-9592. Adm. fee),* where unique pearl-like crystals have formed in cave pools; and **Ohio Caverns** *(2210 State Rte. 245, West Liberty. 937-465-4017. Adm. fee).* The former offers camping on its hundred acres of surface park and some unique accommodations: a covered wagon or cabins on stilts.

Castle Mac-O-Chee, one of the Piatt Castles, West Liberty

West Liberty has some unusual accommodations, too, but you can't stay in them overnight: The **Piatt Castles** ★ *(10051 Twp. Rd. 47. 937-465-2821. April-Oct. daily, March weekends, call for schedule Thanksgiving-Dec.; adm. fee)* were built in the late 1800s by brothers who had been raised here in the Mac-A-Cheek Valley. Abram Piatt's house, Mac-A-Cheek Castle, was used by his descendants until the mid-1980s and contains original furnishings from several eras. Both Abram's castle and Donn Piatt's Mac-O-Chee feature beautiful woodwork and ceiling frescoes.

The route backtracks to Ohio 4 and goes north through farm country to **Marion** *(Convention & Visitors Bureau 614-389-9770 or 800-371-6688),* where Warren G. Harding conducted his 1920 Front Porch Campaign from the Queen Anne **President Warren G. Harding Home and Museum** *(380 Mt. Vernon Ave. 614-387-9630 or 800-600-6894. Mem. Day–Labor Day Wed.-Sun., Sept.-Oct. weekends; adm. fee).* The house is decorated with Harding furnishings; a museum of memorabilia occupies the building behind the house that was used by the press corps during

Harding's campaign. Harding adds to Ohio's reputation for
sending to the White House an impressive number (seven)
of unimpressive Presidents. Harding and his wife, Flo-
rence, are buried in the **Harding Memorial** *(Ohio 423 at Vernon Heights Blvd.)*, a circular monument of Georgian marble.

Popcorn is a big crop around Marion, and the kernels

Bedroom at President Warren G. Harding Home and Museum, Marion

are honored at the **Wyandot Popcorn Museum,** part of
Heritage Hall *(169 E. Church St. 614-387-4255. May-Oct.
Wed.-Sun., Nov.-April weekends).* The evolution of popcorn
machines is shown with working models, and there are
horse-drawn and motorized popcorn wagons. An annual
popcorn festival in early September *(contact Convention &
Visitors Bureau)* features a parade, entertainment, and popcorn in its infinite variety.

Now head south through the town of Delaware to
another interesting cave area, the multilevel ❸ **Olentangy Indian Caverns** *(Olentangy Indian Caverns and
Ohio Frontierland, 1779 Home Rd. 614-548-7917. April-Oct.;
adm. fee),* once used by Indians for refuge and ceremo-
nial purposes.

Backtrack to Delaware, and take Ohio 37 and Ohio 16
into **Newark** *(Convention & Visitors Bureau 614-345-9758).*
The history of human occupancy around Newark goes
back at least to the Hopewell, who erected earthen walls
and an eagle-shaped effigy mound around 2,000 years

ago. Many earthworks were destroyed by the city's expansion, but the **Moundbuilders State Memorial** (*Ohio 79 S of Newark. 614-344-1920. April-Oct.*) protects 66 acres of ancient sites. The memorial's **Ohio Indian Art Museum** (*Mem. Day–Labor Day Wed.-Sun., Sept.-Oct. weekends; adm. fee*) exhibits the work of local prehistoric Indians.

Also in Newark, the **National Heisey Glass Museum** (*W. Church and 6th Sts. 614-345-2932. Closed Mon.; adm. fee*) displays turn-of-the-century pressed ware and hand-cut glass by A.H. Heisey and Co., representing some of eastern Ohio's finest glasswork.

Proceed northeast to **Coshocton,** a canal town that commemorates the bustling trade generated by the Ohio and Erie Canal. At **Historic Roscoe Village** (*100 to 600 blocks of Whitewoman St. 614-622-9310 or 800-877-1830. Adm. fees for some buildings*) some 20 buildings have been restored or re-created to their 1840s look. There are horse-drawn canal rides, craft demonstrations, shops, and lodging.

The village is located along the Muskingum River, which flows south through a beautiful valley to Zanesville. The Western writer Zane Grey was born there, but the town was named after his grandfather, Col. Ebenezer Zane, who hacked a trail through the thick forest that covered the area. Ten miles east of Zanesville awaits the ❹ **National Road–Zane Grey Museum** (*US 22/40 at I-70. 614-872-3143. Daily May-Sept., Wed.-Sat. March-April and Oct.-Nov.; adm. fee*), an odd but interesting mix of Grey's manuscripts and memorabilia and exhibits about the National Road, which was built through here in the 19th century (see sidebar this page). If you want to see endangered animals, detour 20 miles south to the **Wilds** (*14000 International Rd. 614-638-5030. May-Oct.; adm. fee*), where a reclaimed strip mine has become an open-range preserve for southern white rhinos and other endangered species. In addition to guided tours, there is a Visitor Center with a short video on endangered species, conservation efforts, and breeding research.

The route continues east through **Cambridge,** a historic glassmaking center, to **Salt Fork State Park** (*US 22. 614-439-3521*), the state's largest park and a good spot to observe white-tailed deer and beavers. Wildlife has to share space with golfers, powerboats, and a big resort/convention center, but thrives nevertheless.

National Road

Build a road and they will come. That's a truism about Americans that has been accurate for centuries. Back in 1806, Congress decided the best way to shift the young nation's burgeoning population into its new western lands was to build the National Road. The first stretch of gravel ran from Cumberland, Maryland, to the Ohio River at Wheeling, West Virginia; by 1835 it had reached Columbus, Ohio. The road had the desired effect, drawing thousands of wagons out onto the frontier, and spawning a string of cities with inns and shops along the way. Today, US 40 roughly follows the National Road's path.

64

At the National Heisey Glass Museum in Newark

Return to Cambridge and follow I-77 south. From Marietta (you'll return later), follow Ohio 26—dubbed the Covered Bridge Scenic Byway—north into **Wayne National Forest**★ *(Maps and information at Marietta Field Office, Ohio 7, Reno. 614-373-9055. Mon.-Fri.).* You will meet up with the twisting Little Muskingum River and drive through covered bridges. Fall color is brilliant in this corner of Ohio, the river rewards canoeists and fishermen, and a network of seasonal bridle and hiking trails leads into the hollows and up on the peaks.

Take a right on Ohio 800 and a right again on Ohio 7. This twisty route along the Ohio River drops you in ❺ **Marietta** *(Convention & Visitors Bureau 614-373-5178 or 800-288-2577),* once a frontier outpost through which settlers passed on their way into the Northwest Territory. That makes it an appropriate roost for the **Campus Martius, the Museum of the Northwest Territory**★ *(2nd and Washington Sts. 614-373-3750. Daily May-Sept., Wed.-Sun. March-April and Oct.-Nov.; adm. fee).* The Roman name was given to a fortification and government center built by settlers in 1788-1791. You will see Indian crafts, a house from the original fort, and a land office.

Historic Roscoe Village, Coshocton

Also in town find the **Ohio River Museum** *(601 Front St. 614-373-3750. Daily May-Sept., Wed.-Sun. March-April and Oct.-Nov.; adm. fee),* which tells the history of steamboats on the river. A flatboat is on display, along with artifacts from the steamboat days. On the river itself is docked the historic towboat **W.P. Snyder Jr.** Nearby, the **Valley Gem Sternwheeler** *(614-373-7862. June-Aug. Tues.-Sun., May and Sept.-Oct. weekends; adm. fee),* an authentic stern-wheeler, departs for cruises—including fall foliage tours—on the Ohio and Muskingum Rivers.

Head west beyond Athens, to where streams have cut Blackhand sandstone to create beautiful formations in the Hocking Hills—from fern-draped cliffs to recess caves to potholes. **Hocking Hills State Park**★★ *(Ohio 664, SW of Logan. 614-385-6841)* is actually six separate areas, with features that inspired names such as Rock House and Old

Man's Cave. In the 1930s, the Civilian Conservation Corps chipped the steps and dug the tunnels that help hikers along difficult gorge terrain.

The last stops on this route are in the **6** **Chillicothe** vicinity *(Convention & Visitors Bureau 614-775-0900 or 800-413-4118)*. Few locations in North America have so much evidence of prehistoric habitation, and, while the town has a long history as a thriving trade center, residents have done a decent job of preserving evidence of ancient life here. The **Hopewell Culture National Historical Park**★ *(16062 State Rte. 104. 614-774-1125. Adm. fee)* preserves a collection of mounds surrounded by a square embankment. Visitor Center exhibits explore the mystery of the Hopewell people, who prospered from around 200 B.C. to A.D. 500, and display beautiful copperwork and effigy pipes.

Nearby stands the home of Ohio's sixth governor, Thomas Worthington, now preserved as the **Adena State Memorial**★ *(848 Adena Rd. 614-772-1500 or 800-319-7248. Mem. Day–Labor Day Wed.-Sun., Sept.-Oct. weekends; adm. fee).* The modified Georgian 1807 mansion was once the centerpiece of a 25,000-acre farm dotted with gristmills, gardens, and orchards. The spectacular view from the house inspired the design for the Great Seal of Ohio.

Photographer at Old Man's Cave, Hocking Hills State Park

Before heading back to Columbus on US 23, consider catching the melodramatic ***Tecumseb! Outdoor Historical Drama*** *(Sugarloaf Mountain Amphitheater, Delano Marietta Rd. 614-775-0700. Mid-June–Labor Day Mon.-Sat.; adm. fee),* which depicts the life and death of the Shawnee leader, who united the Ohio Valley tribes in opposition to white settlement.

Hollywood Legend

On February 1, 1901, tiny Cadiz became the birthplace of William Clark Gable, the future King of Hollywood. Gable worked at an assortment of odd jobs before he made the big time, including a stint in a tire factory in Akron when he was 14. After finally getting a screen test at MGM, producer Darryl F. Zanuck nixed him, declaring "His ears are too big." Most people remember him for *Gone with the Wind* (1939), but he won his Academy Award for *It Happened One Night* (1934). Though he and his family lived in Cadiz for only a few years, the superstar is far from forgotten. A 7-foot monument stands on Charleston Street, and the Clark Gable Foundation *(614-942-2505)* is busy rebuilding the Gable family home. And each year on the Saturday nearest his birthday, revelers from around the country flock to town to celebrate.

● **345 miles** ● **4 to 5 days** ● **Year-round** ● **Ferries to Lake Erie Islands generally run May through Oct.** ● **Beware of autumn ice storms caused by the "lake effect."**

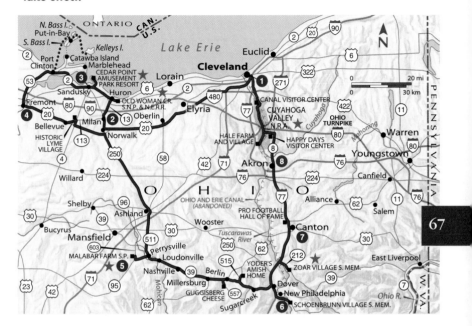

From Ohio's stretch of Lake Erie coast to peaceful Amish farm country and back north to the industrial belt, this northern Ohio journey gives you a lot of different looks, not all of them pretty. The Amish countryside has nostalgic appeal for its horse-and-buggy lifestyle, but this route—embracing Cleveland's ultra-modern Rock and Roll Hall of Fame, the humble birthplace of inventor Thomas Edison, and Akron's marvelous museum of invention—should be viewed as a journey to the modern world.

Cleveland by night

The forward-looking attitude is exemplified by

1 **Cleveland** *(Convention & Visitors Bureau 216-621-4110 or 800-321-1004),* a city that defaulted on its debt only a few decades back. Beginning in the 1980s, Cleveland called off its economic funeral, rejuvenated its old neighborhoods, and brought life to the downtown area with new attractions, including a friendly baseball stadium, restored theaters, and a shrine to loud electric music.

Industry and trade, though, were the historic cornerstones of Cleveland, from the 1827 opening of the Ohio and Erie Canal to the founding of the Standard Oil Company here by John D. Rockefeller in 1870. Today, old industrial haunts along the Cuyahoga River have been converted into tony residential areas—especially the **Historic Warehouse District** *(Bounded by W. 10th and W. 3rd Sts. and Lakeside and Rockwell Aves.)*—and hot nightspots including the **Flats**★ *(Along river bet. Front Ave. and Veterans Memorial Bridge).* The rowdiest nights come after Cleveland Indians home games at **Jacobs Field**★★ *(2401 Ontario St. 216-420-4200. Call for schedule; adm. fee),* beautifully designed with a playing field below street level. The owners don't mind kids watching a few free innings through the pickets by the ticket stiles, since all games are sold out anyway.

Guitarist statue outside Cleveland's Rock and Roll Hall of Fame and Museum

It's an easy walk from the ballfield to the heart of the city: **Public Square** and the **Cuyahoga County Soldiers and Sailors Monument** *(Ontario St. and Superior Ave.),* with a miniature Statue of Liberty atop its granite spire. On one corner of the square rises the 1927 **Terminal Tower;** its observation deck *(adm. fee)* is open on weekends. From the square, walk up Euclid Avenue a few blocks to the **Arcade** *(401 Euclid Ave. 216-621-8500),* a five-story shopping-and-office complex suspended between two office buildings. Built in 1890, and financed in part by John D. Rockefeller, its brass fixtures and beautiful skylight take you back to another time. In the evening, journey farther up Euclid to **Playhouse Square** *(Euclid Ave., bet. 13th and 18th Sts.),* where several classic theaters have been restored and now offer music, dance, and Broadway plays.

In the daytime, the most popular area for Cleveland

visitors is the **North Coast Harbor** *(E. 9th St. Pier, along Lake Erie),* where you can watch sails unfurl among pleasure boats. The 618-foot steamship **_William G. Mather_** *(1001 E. 9th St. Pier. 216-574-6262. Daily Mem. Day–Labor Day, Fri.-Sun. May–Mem. Day and Labor Day–Oct.; adm. fee)* is moored along the dock with maritime exhibits inside. Looking like a giant kids' gizmo of white plastic and glass, the **Great Lakes Science Center**★ *(601 Erieside Ave. 216-694-2000. Adm. fee)* has an attached silver globe housing a six-story surround-sound movie theater.

Right next door looms Cleveland's biggest attraction: the **Rock and Roll Hall of Fame and Museum**★ *(E. 9th St. and Erieside Ave., North Coast Harbor. 216-781-7625 or 800-282-5393. Adm. fee).* Entertaining exhibits trace rock and roll from cotton-field work songs through Elvis, the Temptations, and Bruce Springsteen. Holy relics including Jim Morrison's Cub Scout shirt are on display. Put on headphones to hear Jackson Browne talk about songwriting, or Aretha Franklin reminisce about gospel singing. The shop's mementoes are sparse and overpriced, but for the generation who hoped to die before they got old, it's a nostalgic reminder that the years have, indeed, raced by.

Located in the University Circle area, east of downtown, the world-class **Cleveland Museum of Art**★ *(11150 East Blvd. 216-421-7340. Closed Mon.)* has an outstanding collection of ancient, classical, and modern art, ranging from a Nepalese bronze bodhisattva to Picasso's "La Vie." And the past is preserved at the nearby **Western Reserve Historical Society** *(10825 East Blvd. 216-721-5722. Adm. fee),* which maintains a complex of museums: Two Victorian-era mansions are filled with exhibits on Cleveland's past, and the Frederick C. Crawford Auto-Aviation Museum holds an antique car and aircraft collection. There is also a genealogical library.

Head west from Cleveland on I-71, I-480, Ohio 10, and US 20, then go north on Ohio 58 to **Oberlin** *(Chamber of Commerce, 20 E. College St. 216-774-6262. Mon.-Fri.),* which brought attention to the Fugitive Slave Law when, in 1858, hundreds of citizens ran to rescue fugitive slave John Price, who had been seized by slave hunters on the outskirts of town. Oberlin was a key stop on the Underground Railroad, a loose network of people and houses that smuggled slaves north to freedom (see sidebar page 83). The Chamber of Commerce offers self-guided tour pamphlets of various sites including the 1842 **First Church in Oberlin** *(106 N. Main St.),* where abolitionists met. Peacefully landscaped **Oberlin College** *(Admissions*

Office, 101 N. Professor St. 216-775-8121) was one of the first accredited colleges to graduate women and African Americans. Its world-class music conservatory holds frequent concerts, and there is a wonderful mix of very old and very new art at the **Allen Memorial Art Museum** *(87 N. Main St. 216-775-8665. Closed Mon.; donation).* The musty smell of the stately, high-ceilinged museum comes not from the Cézannes or Monets, but from flaws in the 1917 Cass Gilbert design.

Follow US 20 west and US 250 north through rolling farm country to ❷ **Milan** *(Chamber of Commerce 419-499-2100),* which claims to have once shipped more grain down the Ohio and Erie Canal than any other port except Odessa, in the Ukraine. Trade declined rapidly when railroads bypassed the town in the late 19th century, and today you'll discover a quiet, shady place known primarily as the 1842 birthplace of one of America's greatest inventors. The redbrick **Thomas Edison Birthplace Museum** *(9 Edison Dr. 419-499-2135. Feb.-Nov. Tues.-Sun.; adm. fee)* showcases family furnishings in the Edi-

Thomas Edison Birthplace Museum, Milan

son house, and, next door, some examples of the 1,093 inventions he patented. Down the street, the **Milan Historical Museum** *(10 Edison Dr. 419-499-2968. April-Oct. Tues.-Sun.)* features a video on the canal that made the town's fortunes, plus seven historical buildings including a blacksmith shop and a general store.

The lakeshore to the north is a busy holiday whirl in the summer, but the **Old Woman Creek State Nature Preserve & National Estuarine Research Reserve**★ *(US 6, E of Huron. 419-433-4601. Reserve open daily, Visitor Center open Wed.-Sun.)* is a 571-acre respite from fast food and suntan oil. A barrier beach here has formed an estuary that sustains a variety of plants, waterfowl, fish, and insects. The role of coastal marshes in keeping the Great Lakes healthy is explained at the Visitor Center, and behind it is an observation deck for viewing wildlife on the estuary.

Now the route goes west along US 6, into the busy party atmosphere around ❸ **Sandusky.** Over a century ago, a bright entrepreneur got the idea to rent bathing suits on Cedar Point, a flat sandy finger extending into the lake on Sandusky Bay's east point. That modest enterprise grew into **Cedar Point Amusement Park Resort**★ *(1 Causeway Dr. 419-627-2350. May-Aug. daily, Sept.-Oct. weekends; adm. fee),* which has erected a mountain range of roller-coaster peaks, including the spanking new Mantis, one of the world's highest, fastest, and steepest stand-up roller coasters. There is also an adjacent water park, miniature golf course, and go-cart track. When you need to recover your equilibrium, relax on a sandy beach or in the Hotel Breakers (where six Presidents preceded you).

Motels and fast food joints surround Sandusky, but the town has a quiet, tree-lined center. Here you'll find the **Merry-Go-Round Museum** *(Ohio 6 and Jackson St. 419-626-6111. Daily Mem. Day–Labor Day, Wed.-Sun. Labor Day–Dec. and March–Mem. Day, weekends Jan.-Feb.; adm. fee),* where kids can ride a restored classic carousel while parents examine antique figures and watch a carver create new ones.

West on Ohio 2, **Port Clinton** is a popular takeoff point for the cluster of **Lake Erie Islands**★ ★ *(Visitors Bureau, 109 Madison St. 419-734-4386 or 800-441-1271),* which attract fishermen, birdwatchers, and wine lovers. You can island-hop for a day or spend the night. Some people take their cars, but most rent bicycles or golf carts for getting about. Contact the Visitors Bureau for information on accommodations and ferries, which generally run May through October. (Ferries also leave from Marblehead and Catawba Island.)

The lake's moderating effect makes these islands suitable for grape growing, a fact not lost on the many visitors who come, particularly to **Put-in-Bay** on **South Bass Island,** for some exhaustive wine tasting. Also at Put-in-Bay you'll find **Perry's Victory and International Peace Memorial** *(Late April–late Oct.; fee for elevator),* commemorating Commodore Oliver Hazard Perry's defeat of a British fleet near here during the War of 1812. The monument has a 317-foot observation platform with a good lake view.

Wooden horse head, Merry-Go-Round Museum, Sandusky

Kelleys Island has a winery, too, but it's a quieter scene, and a favorite of birdwatchers and anglers. On the island's north side, at **Kelleys Island State Park**★ *(Park office, end of Division St. 419-746-2546),* look for rare glacial grooves—smooth troughs of limestone embedded with ancient fossils. Glaciers dug these grooves over 20,000 years ago; sadly, quarrying destroyed much larger examples earlier this century, and weather is smoothing what's left. The weather has been even harder on **Inscription Rock** (*Lakeshore Dr. and Addison St.*), where centuries ago Native Americans carved petroglyphs of animals and men. The images are faint now, but a display re-creates the originals.

Back ashore, the route turns south on Ohio 53 and inland, to ❹ **Fremont** and the **Rutherford B. Hayes Presidential Center** (*1337 Hayes Ave. 419-332-2081 or 800-998-7737. Library closed Sun.; adm. fee*). Hayes' 33-room Victorian mansion at Spiegel Grove has been paired with a grandiose museum.

Down the road on US 20, just east of Bellevue, **Historic Lyme Village** (*5487 Ohio 113 E. 419-483-4949. Tues.-Sun. June-Aug., Sun. May and Sept.; adm. fee*) features a collection of restored buildings ranging from pioneer log houses to an 1882 Second Empire mansion, complete with a museum. The **Postmark Colletors Museum** in the Old Lyme Post Office exhibits unique postmarks from the world-renowned collections of the Postmark Collectors Club, headquartered here (see sidebar this page).

Heading southeast on US 20 and US 250 to Ashland, south on Ohio 511 to Perrysville, west on Ohio 95, and north on Ohio 603, the drive now dips through some of Ohio's most productive farmland. It was to this country that Pulitzer Prize-winning author Louis Bromfield came to test his ideas about productive farming and conservation at ❺ **Malabar Farm State Park**★ (*Off Ohio 603. 419-892-2784. Mem. Day–Labor Day daily, Labor Day–Mem. Day Tues.-Sun.; adm. fee*). The 32-room country home is not your usual farmhouse—there are bookshelves everywhere, a luxurious dining room, and spacious staircases and studies. Though it's now a state park, the farm still raises cattle and hens using Bromfield's techniques. Visitors, however, may be more interested in seeing the room where Humphrey Bogart and Lauren Bacall honeymooned in 1945. Down the park road stands the **Malabar Inn** (*3645 Pleasant Valley Rd. 419-938-5205. Daily Mem. Day–Labor Day, Tues.-Sun. April–Mem. Day and Labor Day–Dec.*), a restaurant housed in an 1820 brick building.

Originally from Switzerland, the Amish came to Ohio in the early 19th century looking for a place where they could follow their strict Anabaptist-derived beliefs. They still shun cars and electricity, but they're quite accustomed to gawking sight-seers. For a glimpse into their

---

Postmarks

An old post office that was taking a beating as a chicken coop now holds a museum that displays the wares of the Postmark Collectors Club at **Historic Lyme Village**. "It's not the stamps," says museum curator Vick Steward with a hint of exasperation. "It's the *cancel*." He pulls out rare postmarks from 19th-century Massachusetts, stored in acid-free plastic. To hear club members tell it, universities and museums have begged for this collection, but the club doesn't want to relinquish control. Postmarks go back as far as the mid-17th century—before that, a postmaster just drew a line through a stamp or wrote his name across it. Are there postmarks that collectors would die for? There is one they'd especially like to have: a postmark from New Salem, Illinois, in the 1830s...for three years the postmaster there was a young fellow named Abraham Lincoln.

72

world backtrack to Perrysville and drive east along Ohio 39, through beautiful farmland. In the towns of **Millersburg, Berlin,** and **Sugarcreek,** numerous restaurants specialize in Amish fare, which is generally simple, heavy, and nourishing. Many stores sell Amish-made furniture, quilts, and other merchandise. To learn about the origins and beliefs of the Amish and the Mennonites, another Swiss sect, stop in Berlin at the **Mennonite Information Center**★ *(5798 Cty. Rd. 77, off Ohio 39. 330-893-3192. Mon.-Sat.; fee for cyclorama),* which tells the story with a colorful panoramic cyclorama (a large circular mural) titled "Behalt."

Beyond Berlin, Amish buggies deliver morning milk to **Guggisberg Cheese** *(5060 Ohio 557, off Ohio 39. 330-893-2500. Cheesemaking Mon.-Fri. a.m.)* to make wheels of baby Swiss. The Amish way of life is demonstrated farther east at **Yoder's Amish Home** *(6050 Ohio 515, off Ohio 39. 330-893-2541. Mid-April–Oct. Mon.-Sat.; adm. fee),* a working farm; locals, however, note that Eli Yoder was raised in an Amish family but never baptized into the faith.

Amish horse and buggy along Ohio 39

Before the Amish, the Delaware Indians came to this area, pushed by European settlers and other tribes to the **New Philadelphia** vicinity. In 1772 Moravian missionaries hoping to convert the Delaware built what's now the ❻ **Schoenbrunn Village State Memorial** *(E. High Ave./Ohio 259. 216-339-3636 or 800-752-2711. Mem. Day–Labor Day daily, Labor Day–Oct. weekends; adm. fee).* The linear village of simple log structures, which was abandoned within five years, has been reconstructed.

Next head north on I-77, stopping at another experimental Christian community, historic **Zoar Village State Memorial**★ *(3 miles SE of I-77, on Ohio 212. 330-874-3011 or 800-262-6195. Wed.-Sun. Mem. Day–Labor Day, Sat.-Sun. April–Mem. Day and Labor Day–Oct.; adm. fee).* A commune of German Separatists arrived here in 1817, vowing to pool their labor, land, and assets. The group was very successful until their charismatic leader, Joseph Bimeler, died; it disbanded late in the 19th century. Centered around the geometric-shaped Zoar Garden, many of the town's restored buildings are open for tours.

The route moves north to **7** **Canton** *(Visitors Bureau 330-454-1439 or 800-533-4302)*, where the nation's 25th President, William McKinley, is entombed at the **McKinley National Memorial** *(800 McKinley Monument Dr. N.W. 330-455-7043. Adm. fee to museum)*. McKinley may not be remembered for his Front Porch Campaign or his support of the gold standard, which may explain why the adjacent **McKinley Museum** is mostly a kids' science discovery center with a planetarium and just some McKinley memorabilia. Canton is also home to the **Pro Football Hall of Fame** *(2121 George Halas Dr. N.W. 330-456-8207. Adm. fee)*, which will fascinate football fans with its statuary of sports greats, replays of Super Bowl games, and mementoes. Non-fans dragged along will probably want to punt the football-shaped roof all the way to Youngstown.

Amish farm, near Nashville

That's a long way east, but an excursion along US 62 is worth the detour if you appreciate American art. The definitive collection at the **Butler Institute of American Art** ★ *(524 Wick Ave., Youngstown. 330-743-1107. Closed Mon.; adm. fee)* ranges from early Albert Bierstadt landscapes to John Singleton Copley portraits to moody Edward Hopper city scenes. A growing contemporary art collection is housed in the post-modern West Wing.

From Canton, the drive proceeds north on I-77 to **8** **Akron** *(Chamber of Commerce 330-376-5550)*, which, contrary to its gritty image, is in fact a city of considerable charm. Like many others, the town was seeded by the Ohio and Erie Canal, but its growth was powered by an unlikely industrial tandem: oatmeal and rubber. The Akron Milling Company (which later became part of Quaker Oats) sold oatmeal to Civil War armies; the old Quaker factory is now an appealing downtown shopping-

and-entertainment complex. And the Goodrich and Goodyear rubber companies took off with the advent of the automobile. The Goodyear plant maintains a somewhat dated exhibit called the **Goodyear World of Rubber** *(1201 E. Market St. 330-796-7117. Mon.-Fri.),* which explains the production of natural and synthetic rubber.

Ponder that notion during a visit to **Inventure Place**★★ *(221 S. Broadway St. 330-762-6565 or 800-968-4332. Closed Mon. Labor Day–Feb.; adm. fee),* which celebrates great American inventors and delves into their methods and thought processes. A series of interactive workstations let kids of all ages take apart a computer, play a stringless harp, or try their hand at inventing the next synthetic material.

Akron's early wealth is lavishly displayed at the beautiful **Stan Hywet Hall and Gardens**★ *(714 N. Portage Path. 330-836-5533. April-Dec. daily, Jan.-March Tues.-Sun.; adm. fee).* Built by Goodyear cofounder F.A. Seiberling, the 65-room Tudor Revival mansion is surrounded by 70 acres of land-scaped grounds.

Returning to Cleveland, take Ohio 8 and Ohio 303 through the **Cuyahoga Valley National Recre-ation Area**★ *(Happy Days Visitor Center, off Ohio 303. 440-526-5256),* a 22-mile preserve that follows the old Ohio and Erie Canal. At the

Jim Thorpe statue at Canton's Pro Football Hall of Fame

valley's south end awaits **Hale Farm and Village** *(2686 Oak Hill Rd. 330-666-3711. Late May–Oct. Tues.-Sun.; adm. fee),* a mid-19th-century living history museum that depicts life in the Western Reserve. Artisans blow glass and spin wool, and blacksmiths work the forge; there are also orchards, a schoolhouse, and a steam-powered sawmill. The workings of the canal and its key role historically in Ohio's economy are explored in exhibits at the **Canal Vis-itor Center** *(Hillside and Canal Rds.).* Visitors can hoof it along the old towpath, or take a variety of trips starting at the valley's north end aboard the **Cuyahoga Valley Scenic Railroad**★ *(1630 W. Mill St., Peninsula. 216-657-2000. Mem. Day–Labor Day Wed.-Sun., Labor Day–Mem. Day weekends, closed Jan.; adm. fee),* particularly good for fall-color trips.

Historic Passages

● **400 miles** ● **2 to 3 days** ● **Year-round** ● **Photo identification with proof of citizenship but no passport required at Canadian border.**

At first glance, this might be called the Rust Road—it's a tour of industrial Michigan, from the line of freighters slipping by Port Huron, to the auto assembly lines of gritty Flint, to the inner-city neighborhoods of hard-luck Detroit. But look again. Between Port Huron and Flint lie lands dotted with fertile farms. Top-ranked universities reside within East Lansing and Ann Arbor. And Detroit and southwest Ontario share historical significance, having been a major pathway for slaves escaping to freedom on the Underground Railroad.

Beginning in Port Huron, the drive explores Flint and a pair of rival college towns. The tour continues on to Dearborn, where Henry Ford's factories began churning out Model Ts in the early 1900s. After Detroit's zesty culture is explored, the route jumps across the Canadian border at Windsor, crossing flat farmlands to Point Pelee National Park in southwest Ontario. A visit to the Uncle Tom's Cabin Historic Site completes the drive.

A favored site since the 17th century, ❶ **Port Huron** *(Convention & Visitors Bureau 810-987-8687 or 800-852-4242)* is where the French built Fort St. Joseph, to keep an eye on any Brits who might try to sneak into French territories to the north. Americans built Fort Gratiot on the site of the French fort in 1814; this history is described in an exhibit at the **Port Huron Museum** *(1115 6th St. 810-982-0891. Wed.-Sun.; adm. fee)*. The museum also features Indian artifacts, an exhibit on inventor Thomas Edison's boyhood in Port Huron, and items salvaged from Lake Huron shipwrecks. From the soaring **Blue Water Bridge** you get a panoramic view of the lake where the ships went down. Today its surface is dotted with freighters funneling down the St. Clair River toward Lake Erie. Walkers can cross the span *(mid-March–mid-Oct.)*, lingering at the high point 160 feet above the water. Modern freighters rely on sophisticated navigation tools such as radar, but they also keep an eye on the beacon of the 19th-century **Fort Gratiot Lighthouse** *(Lighthouse Park. 810-984-2424. Mem. Day–Labor Day Wed.-Sun.)*.

Driving west on I-69 from Port Huron toward Flint, the route passes bountiful farms, many of which sell cider and fresh fruit. Visitors can also gather their own blue-berries in the summer, and raspberries until autumn. To locate farms that welcome pickers, request a **Farm Market and U-Pick Directory** from the Michigan Department of Agriculture *(P.O. Box 30017, Lansing, MI 48909)*.

❷ **Flint** *(Convention & Visitors Bureau 810-232-8900 or 800-25-FLINT)* may never entirely recover from Michael Moore's documentary, **"Roger & Me"** (1989), which skewered General Motors and made Moore's hometown look like a throwaway in the auto industry's merciless restructuring during the 1980s. But the city is not dead, and the wounds appear to be healing. It may surprise some to learn that they're still making vehicles, at the **GM Truck and Bus Flint Assembly Plant** *(Van Slyke and Bristol Rds. 810-236-0893. Mon.-Fri. Reservations required)*, which you can tour.

Another measure of the city's vitality, the **Flint Cultural Center** *(810-760-1087)*, a cluster of boxy modern buildings bisected by East Kearsley Street, includes **Whiting Auditorium** *(1241 E. Kearsley St. 810-760-1138)* for the Flint Symphony Orchestra and other performers; and the **Alfred P. Sloan Museum** *(1221 E. Kearsley St. 810-760-1169. Adm. fee)*, which describes the area's rich history, including the birth of GM. The museum also has vintage cars, and newsreels reporting the famous (and violent) strike in 1937 that marked the rise of the United Auto Workers.

Thomas Edison exhibit, Port Huron Museum

Also at the cultural center you'll find the **Flint Institute of Arts**★ *(1120 E. Kearsley St. 810-234-1695. Closed Mon.),* housing an impressive collection ranging from 17th-century French tapestries to mobiles by modernist Alexander Calder, with some fine regional work as well.

There was life before the automobile in this area, some of it re-created at **Crossroads Village and Huckleberry Railroad** *(6140 Bray Rd. 810-736-7100 or 800-648-PARK. Mid-May–Labor Day daily, Sept. weekends, selected days in Oct. and Dec.; adm. fee).* You can hop on a steam locomotive, take a ride on a paddle wheeler on Mott Lake, or join in the busy 19th-century village scene, where there is an operating gristmill, blacksmith shop, cider press, and Ferris wheel.

The route continues southwest on I-69 to **East Lansing** *(Convention & Visitors Bureau 517-487-6800 or 800-968-8474),* a town so oriented to **Michigan State University** *(517-355-1855)* that its downtown area runs along the school's northern perimeter. One of the nation's first land-grant colleges, MSU's stately old campus buildings are surrounded by spreading oaks, thick lawns, and blooming bushes. The monoliths of the newer campus have been enlivened by

Football fever, Spartan Stadium, Michigan State University in East Lansing

horticulturists, and the extensive **W.J. Beal Botanical Garden** *(W. Circle Dr. 517-355- 9582. Self-guided tours, or guided tours for fee)* features plants from poison ivy and hemp to peonies. Continue to the **Botany Greenhouses**★ *(E. Circle Dr. by Farm Ln. 517-355-0229. Self-guided tours, or guided tours for fee),* highlighted by the **Butterfly House,** where the delicate creatures flit amid hibiscus and other flowers. Top off the visit with a stop for student-made ice cream at the **Dairy Store** *(Anthony Hall, Farm Ln. 517-355-8466. March-Oct. daily, Nov.-Feb. Mon.-Sat.).* The university also has a small art collection at the **Kresge Art Museum** *(Auditorium and Physics Rds. 517-355-7631. Closed Aug.)* and a skyful of stars at the **Abrams Planetarium** *(Science Rd. and Shaw Ln. 517-355-4672. Sept.–late July Fri.-Sun.; adm. fee).*

Now proceed to ❸ **Lansing** *(Convention & Visitors Bureau 517-487-6800 or 800-968-8474).* The city was no more than a few cabins in the woods when it was made the state capital in 1847, in part because the old capital, Detroit, was too vulnerable to attack from Canada. The state government brought people, but it was the production of Ransom E. Olds's automobiles that really built the town.

The Olds Curved Dash runabout was the world's most popular car in 1905, and you can see the evolution of Oldsmobile models at the **R. E. Olds Transportation Museum** *(240 Museum Dr. 517-372-0422. Adm. fee)*. You'll discover here that the original REO Speedwagon rolled rather than rocked. The Olds facility is one of a cluster of museums in renovated warehouses along the Grand River, part of the 6-mile **Riverfront Park and Trail.** Nearby **Impression 5** *(200 Museum Dr. 517-485-8116. Adm. fee)* is a big two-story kids' space, with computer stations and a big heart you can walk through (the valves are pink swinging doors). The adjacent **Michigan Museum of Surveying** *(220 Museum Dr. 517-484-6605. Mon.-Fri.)* has a small collection of equipment dating from the 19th century, and exhibits on the arduous but essential task of early surveyors.

Many of the themes scattered in the previous museums are pulled together in the **Michigan Historical Museum**★ *(717 W. Allegan St. 517-373-3559)*, a nifty modern building of banded granite, limestone, and copper erected around a tall white pine. Inside are first-rate exhibits on Michigan's culture, geology, and natural history. You can stroll down a 1920s street, "drop" into an Upper Peninsula copper mine, and view some big-finned beauties from the 1957 Detroit Auto Show. The only Lansing building that can compete with the museum is the 1879 **State Capitol**★ *(Capitol and Michigan Aves. 517-373-2353. Mon.-Sat.)*, with its ornate cornices and dome, designed to resemble the federal Capitol. Visitors can watch from the balcony as legislators orate, or take a free tour.

Resume the drive by going east on I-96 and south on US 23 to ❹ **Ann Arbor**★ *(Convention & Visitors Bureau 313-995-7281 or 800-888-9487)*, home of the University of Michigan and the Wolverines. Here you'll find a university town par excellence—a campus bursting with athletic and intellectual fervor, as well as terrific bookstores, and good food and entertainment.

The heart of the **University of Michigan** *(313-764-1817)* abuts the busy stores, movie houses, and coffee

Student Union, University of Michigan in Ann Arbor

shops of State Street, but the tentacles of the campus extend throughout the community. Just off the center of campus stands the Greek Revival **University of Michigan Museum of Art** *(525 S. State St. 313-764-0395. Closed Mon.),* where extensive collections supply rotating exhibits ranging from sixth-century Byzantine sculpture to paintings by Picasso, Whistler, and Monet, and photographs by Ansel Adams. The museum's Asian art collection is also first-rate. Nearby stands the intimate **Kelsey Museum of Archaeology** ★ *(434 S. State St. 313-764-9304. May–Labor Day Tues.-Sun.),* which displays artifacts drawn from the ancient Mediterranean, many from U of M excavations. The collection includes Roman funerary stones and Egyptian mummy masks. Dinosaur bones are a staple of natural history museums, but the **Exhibit Museum of Natural History** ★ *(1109 Geddes Ave. 313-764-0478)* has some of the biggest and best in the Midwest, led by a gape-jawed *Allosaurus*. The museum depicts different prehistoric eras in dioramas, and has exhibits about the stars, the human body, and Native Americans. Also worth a visit is the **Law Quadrangle,** a cloister of ivy-covered, Gothic buildings (modeled after English universities), with an underground library addition.

On the southwest edge of campus stands the 102,501-seat **Michigan Stadium** ★ *(Stadium Blvd. and Main St. 313-764-1817),* dug down into the ground so that street level entry nearly puts you at the uppermost seats.

The North Campus has a completely different feel: roomier, quieter, and a bit sterile, with blocky buildings designed by architect Eero Saarinen in the 1950s. The impressive **Stearns Collection of Musical Instruments** *(Moore Bldg., 1100 Bates Dr. 313-763-4389. Wed.-Sun.)* contains rare traditional noisemakers from all over the world.

At the Henry Ford Museum, Dearborn

There is life off campus, too, from the excellent and expanding **Ann Arbor Hands-On Museum** *(219 E. Huron St. 313-995-5437. Closed Mon.; adm. fee)* for children of all ages, to the **Michigan Theater** *(603 E. Liberty St. 313-668-8397. Adm. fee),* a grand 1928 cinema house now used for art films, concerts, and occasional silent movies accompanied by an original Barton organ.

Now the drive proceeds to **Dearborn** *(Convention & Visitors Bureau 313-259-4333).* It should come as no surprise that the the city's entry in the "world's largest" competition is a tire, a towering Uniroyal wheel that stands next to I-94 as you enter the epicenter of the nation's automobile culture.

Begin with the **Henry Ford Estate–Fair Lane** ★ *(4901 Evergreen Rd., bet. Hubbard Dr. and US 12. 313-593-5590. April-Dec. daily, Jan.-March Sun.-Fri.; adm. fee),* Henry Ford's rather stunted castle on the River Rouge, surrounded by beautiful grounds that screen out the suburban clamor

Greenfield Village, Dearborn

nearby. Though Ford originally wanted a home in the Frank Lloyd Wright Prairie School style, he had Elizabethan and other design elements added. Carved wood paneling, Wedgwood fireplaces, and wrought-iron gates reflect an opulent lifestyle. More interesting is Ford's rustic basement Field Room, where he hung out with Thomas Edison and naturalist John Burroughs. Outdoors, the well-known landscape architect Jens Jensen created the flowery grottoes, cascades, and long, shady meadows along the River Rouge. Fair Lane also has its own innovative hydroelectric powerhouse, still full of machinery.

Nearby is the **Henry Ford Museum** *(20900 Oakwood Blvd. 313-271-1620. Adm. fee),* housing a comprehensive collection of historic vehicles lined up on a curving chronological "highway." The museum goes beyond the evolution of car design to show how the automobile reshaped American lives. Ford himself played no small role in this revolution, and his life is chronicled as well.

Ford's interest in American invention and innovation is the guiding light of both the museum and the adjacent **Greenfield Village**★★ *(Closed Jan.-March; adm. fee)*, an 81-acre park where Ford gathered buildings in which brilliant American inventors have worked: Thomas Edison's

Night lights of Detroit

laboratory, the study where Noah Webster wrote his dictionary, the Wright brothers' cycle shop, among many others. It's a cut above most nostalgic Americana theme parks, because most of the houses, shops, and farm activities are genuine. There's fun, too, with train rides, a 1913 carousel, and seasonal festivals where visitors get to join in traditional activities. Try a little 19th-century road fare at the **Eagle Tavern** *(Closed Jan.-March and Nov. Mon.-Thurs.)*, before you remount your horse (or Bronco).

From Dearborn take US 12 to ❺ **Detroit** *(Convention & Visitors Bureau 313-259-4333 or 800-DETROIT)*. The people who came to work in auto factories—particularly African Americans and Arab immigrants—swelled the population of the city in the early 20th century. Later, in the 1960s and 1970s, the city was beset by factory layoffs, racial conflict, and suburban flight. Old Detroiters admit that visitors still have their doubts about the city, and there are still blighted areas. But boosters point to evidence that the city is making a comeback: Some of the beautiful old downtown buildings have been restored—the 1929 **Guardian Building**★ *(Griswold and Congress Sts.)*, with colorful Aztec patterns in its art deco design; and the popular 1928 concert hall, **Fox Theatre** ★ *(Woodward Ave. and Montcalm St. 313-983-6611. Adm. fee)*, with a decorative interior of lions, Greek masks, peacocks, and Buddhas. Newer office buildings such as the dark cluster of cylinders that make up the **Renaissance Center** *(E. Jefferson Ave. and Brush St. 313-568-5600)* have won fewer hearts, but they represent a comeback for the downtown waterfront. Take the elevator to the **Summit Observation Deck** *(313-568-8000. Adm. fee)* on the 73rd floor for a panoramic view of the city, Canada, and Lake St. Clair.

To see the city up close, try the inexpensive **Detroit People Mover** ★ *(13 stops downtown. 313-962-RAIL. Fare)*, which makes a 2.9-mile loop around the city center, including a section along the Detroit River. Each station is decorated with specially commissioned art. You can also see the city from tour boats aboard **Diamond Jack's River Tours** *(Hart Plaza. 313-843-7676. Late May–Aug. Tues.-Sun., Sept. Fri.-Sun.; fare)*, a two-hour narrated journey that loops around Belle Isle.

Now drive north on Woodward Avenue for some of Detroit's cultural treasures. The magnificent **Detroit Institute of Arts** ★ *(5200 Woodward Ave. 313-833-7900. Wed.-Sun.; adm. fee)* holds a vast collection acquired during Detroit's boom years. Though funding problems now limit the hours, the European greats are all here, from Rembrandt to Matisse. Less famous, but equally fascinating, are items such as Islamic calligraphy, and an initiation mask from Africa's Kuba people. The great Mexican muralist Diego Rivera created a series of compelling frescoes, "Detroit Industry," for the DIA.

The **Detroit Historical Museums** ★ *(5401 Woodward Ave. 313-833-1805. Wed.-Sun.; adm. fee)* have exhibits on the history of cars in Detroit (including a working "car drop," in which a Cadillac body drops onto a chassis); other products Detroit workers made in the 18th and 19th centuries; and Detroit's role as the last stop before Canada on the Underground Railroad (see sidebar this page). There's also an enormous toy train collection for the kids.

The highlight of this district is the recently opened **Museum of African American History** ★★

Underground Railroad

There were no tracks or tunnels, no engineers or Pullman cars, but the Underground Railroad ferried thousands of slaves to freedom before and during the Civil War. The "railroad" was a clandestine network of safe houses between the South and North where runaway bondsmen and women could hide. When the Fugitive Slave Law of 1850 required slaves in the North be returned to southern owners, the "stations" of the railroad extended into Canada. The best overview of the Underground Railroad is found in the vivid and informative displays at Detroit's **Museum of African American History** (315 E. Warren Ave. 313-494-5800).

83

(315 E. Warren Ave. 313-494-5800. Closed Mon.; adm. fee), beautifully designed with a dome of tinted glass resembling the peaks of African village huts. Crossing a bridge to reach historical exhibits, you peer into a reproduction of an incredibly cramped slave ship. The fresh scholarship and insight of the exhibits has an exhilarating effect—how many of us know of the African emperor of Mali, Mansa Musa, who sent sailors west across the sea to a new land in the 14th century?

Motown Historical Museum, Detroit

If this is the heart of Detroit, the soul is a few minutes away, at the **Motown Historical Museum★** *(2648 W. Grand Blvd. 313-875-2264. Adm. fee),* in the small house where Berry Gordy started the record company Motown and recorded a roster of artists including the Supremes, Smokey Robinson, the Temptations, and the Jackson Five. The sequin costumes and primitive recording studio are downstairs; the Gordy family apartment is re-created upstairs.

Gordy has long since moved on to finer digs, just like the big wheels of the auto industry did when their fortunes were made. Generally, they moved up the Detroit River shoreline, to various wealthy enclaves such as **Grosse Pointe Shores.** Take Jefferson Avenue, which becomes Lake Shore Drive, northeast to the **Edsel and Eleanor Ford House★** *(1100 Lake Shore Dr. 313-884-4222. April-Dec. Tues.-Sun., Jan.-March Wed.-Sun.; adm. fee),* the 1929 English country house of Henry's son, Edsel, and his philanthropist wife, Eleanor. After the one-hour house tour, you can spend time wandering the beautiful grounds, pool house, and playhouse, a miniaturized version of a Tudor-style house.

Backtrack to **Belle Isle** *(MacArthur Bridge at E. Grand Blvd. 313-852-4075)* for an easy urban escape. Locals take R and R on the island by enjoying its picnic areas, nature trails, and fishing piers, as well as a popular zoo and aquarium. Some summer weekends, it gets a little crowded. On the island's southwestern end, facing Detroit, stands the white marble **Scott Fountain.** Nearby rests the **Dossin Great Lakes Museum** *(100 Strand Dr. 313-852-4051. Wed.-Sun.; adm. fee),* with exhibits on the Great Lakes and the shipping industry, including a luxurious steamer smoking lounge and a freighter pilot-house with a view of passing boats on the Detroit River. Two hundred acres of wetland forest with walking trails sprawl across the island's middle—you might even see deer here. The **Belle Isle Nature Center** *(Oakway Trail and Lake Side Dr. 313-852-4056. Closed Mon.)* lies nearby at the island's northeast end. Now recross the bridge and drive west toward downtown.

Here the tour makes a hop to Canada: Take the soaring, 2-mile Ambassador Bridge over the river to Detroit's Canadian twin city, Windsor. Visitors to Canada must have proof of citizenship—either a passport or a birth certificate and photo identification. Parents should have their children's birth certificates in hand. Traffic can be thick coming and going across the Detroit River border.

Windsor *(Convention & Visitors Bureau 519-255-6530 or 800-265-3633)* is so oriented toward Detroit you hardly know you've left the United States. The symbiotic relationship intensified during Prohibition, when distilleries in Windsor supplied speakeasies in Detroit with illegal hooch. Today, similarly, Detroiters cross to Windsor to indulge their gambling urges at numerous bingo halls and 24-hour gaming venues, including the expanding **Casino Windsor**

(445 Riverside Dr. W. 519-258-7878 or 800-991-7777) and the paddle wheeler ***Northern Belle*** Casino *(350 Riverside Dr. E. 519-258-7878 or 800-991-7777).* Nearby awaits **Windsor's Community Museum** *(254 Pitt St. W. 519-253-1812. May-Sept. Tues.-Sun., Oct.-April Tues.-Sat.),* built in 1812.

Peace Fountain, Detroit River

Much of Windsor's riverfront is protected from development by a series of parks. There's also a spectacular light-and-water display at the **Peace Fountain** *(Coventry Gardens, Riverside Dr. and Pilette Rd. May-Oct.),* situated just offshore in the Detroit River. Across town, the collection at the **Art Gallery of Windsor** *(Devonshire Mall, 3100 Howard Ave. 519-969-4494. Closed Mon.)* emphasizes Canadian artists and subjects from the mid-18th century forward. It's located in a mall, but it takes its mission seriously.

It's a short journey south on Highway 18 to **Amherstburg,** home of **Fort Malden National Historic Site** ★ *(100 Laird Ave. 519-736-5416. Adm. fee),* the remnants of a fort with a beautiful riverside setting. The original fort, built by the British in 1796, was destroyed as they retreated during the War of 1812. It was later rebuilt during the Upper Canada Rebellion of 1837. The **North American Black Historical Museum and Cultural Centre** *(277 King St. 519-736-5434. April-Nov. Wed.-Sun.; adm. fee)* is a work in progress, following the journey of Africans to North America, often as slaves, and then north to freedom via the Underground Railroad in the 19th century. Many blacks first tasted freedom after crossing the Detroit River to Amherstburg. The work of contemporary black artists is exhibited on the second floor.

Travel east on Route 18 to the **Southwestern Ontario Heritage Village** *(6155 Rte. 23. 519-776-6909. July-Aug. daily, April–mid-Nov. Wed.-Sun.; adm. fee),* a collection of 19th-century buildings set in flat farm- and woodland. During the summer, costumed interpreters offer tours of the village, including the church, schoolhouse, and general store.

Continue toward Point Pelee. If it's spring or late fall, stop on the way at the **Jack Miner Sanctuary** *(3rd Concession, W of Rte. 29, Kingsville. 519-733-4034. Mon.-Sat.)* to see huge flocks of Canada geese making a rest stop on their migration north or south. Birding is a rewarding adventure in southwest Ontario, an avian crossroads dotted with marshes and woodlands. The sanctuary has a Nature Center and a pond where kids can hand-feed birds.

Southwestern Ontario Heritage Village

Now proceed to ❻ **Point Pelee National Park** ★ ★ *(R.R. 1, Leamington. 519-322-2371. Adm. fee),* another favorite birding site—and much more. Visitors can hike the sandy tip that sticks into the waters of Lake Erie (you can swim, too, if it's not too cold and windy), explore the marshes by boardwalk or water *(park canoe rentals April-Oct.),* bicycle *(rentals April-Oct.),* and learn about the lake and the park's ecosystem from naturalists and exhibits at the Visitor Center. If you come in the winter—when you can cross-country ski and ice skate in the park—the ice jams around the tip are worth seeing.

If the tip has whetted your appetite for the lake, take a

ferry *(519-724-2115 or 800-661-2220. Fare)* from Leamington to Pelee Island, where you can visit the **Pelee Island Heritage Centre** *(West Dock. 519-724-2291. May–mid-Nov.; adm. fee)* to learn about paleontology, archaeology, fishing, and lake shipwrecks. The island is also home to a thriving vineyard, the wares of which can be sampled at the **Pelee Island**

Marsh boardwalk at Point Pelee National Park, Ontario

Wine Pavillion *(20 East-West Rd. 519-724-2469. May-Oct.).*

Continue to **7** **North Buxton,** where the **Buxton Historic Site & Museum** *(Rte. 6/ADShad Rd. 519-352-4799. May-Sept. Wed.-Sun.; adm. fee)* was another key site on the Underground Railroad. It was here that former slaves put down roots in the 1850s as part of the Elgin Settlement. The community thrived, and descendants of the original settlers have stocked a museum with artifacts. There's also an 1861 school building commemorating the settlers' academic success.

Zigzag north to **Uncle Tom's Cabin Historic Site** *(R.R. 5, at end of Park St., Dresden. 519-683-2978. Mid-May–mid-Oct., closed some Mon.).* Josiah Henson escaped to Canada in 1830 after being enslaved for 40 years. His story helped inspire Harriet Beecher Stowe's classic novel, *Uncle Tom's Cabin.* A church, houses, and exhibits on the journey of Henson and others are on display.

Now drive north and west to Sarnia, where you make a short hop back to Port Huron over the Blue Water Bridge.

Along Lake Michigan★

● 290 miles ● 2 days ● Spring through autumn ● Pierce Stocking Scenic Drive closes mid-Nov.–March.

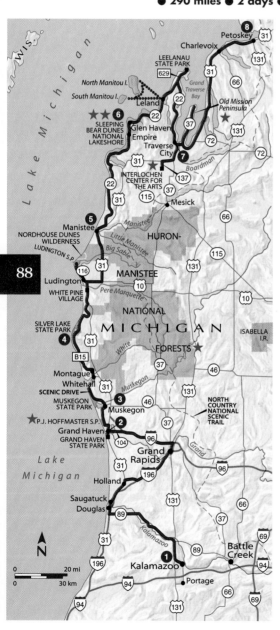

No state in the union has as much freshwater shoreline as Michigan, and no place in the world can match the freshwater sand dunes that drift inland in mammoth mounds along the state's western edge. This route follows the Lake Michigan shoreline north along those dunes, stopping at hilly harbors and orchard farms that have long served as retreats for the well-to-do from Grand Rapids and Chicago.

Some hundred years ago, the coast bustled with ships hauling timber from the huge forests of Michigan, and factory stacks rose like weeds along the harbors. Some still stand, but they are mostly smokeless monuments to a productive but ravenous past. What remains are the cooling breezes off the lake, the beautiful dunes and rejuvenated forest, and harbors crammed with fishing and pleasure boats. This route begins with visits to well-groomed inland towns, Kalamazoo and Grand Rapids, and then hugs the shoreline as it journeys north, pausing at historic fishing villages and natural preserves along the way.

Despite its loopy name—an Indian derivation referring to bubbling springs—❶ **Kalamazoo** *(Chamber of Commerce 616-381-4000)* has a reputation for middle America simplicity, with neat parks and shopping malls and tree-shaded neighborhoods. At the **Kalamazoo Aviation History Museum**★ *(3101 E. Milham Rd. 616-382-*

6555. April-Aug.; adm. fee), visitors can strap into the cockpit of an F-80 Shooting Star or one of five other pilot seats for a simulated ride. In the summer, watch technicians working at the restoration center to keep the old planes in running order. Weather permitting, there is a demonstration Flight of the Day.

Celery was the mainstay of farmers in Kalamazoo County when they began reclaiming marshlands in the 1850s, and this unprepossessing vegetable gets top billing at the **Celery Flats Interpretive Center** *(7335 Garden Ln., Portage. 616-329-4518. May-Sept. Fri.-Sun.; fee for tours).* Old buildings at the site include a one-room schoolhouse and an 1846 manor, and in August you can chew on celery sticks fresh from the gardens.

Heading northwest toward the lake, you'll spot the twin towns of **Douglas** and **Saugatuck** arrayed around the Kalamazoo River, where it slows to form Lake Kalamazoo. The area is a self-described artists' retreat, its waterside dotted with cozy bungalows and rickety little docks. The mammoth **SS Keewatin** *(Harbour Village, Blue Star Mem. Hwy. and Union St. 616-857-2107. May-Sept. daily, Oct. weekends; adm. fee),* docked nearby, is a survivor of the passenger steamship era. While the exterior is a bit rusty, a sign reassures: "Yes! She is floating"; the museum inside features the luxurious trappings of lake travel a century ago. Landlubbers may prefer bouncy overland sight-seeing in the open-air "dune schooners" of **Saugatuck Dune Rides** *(Blue Star Mem. Hwy., 0.5 mile N of I-96. 616-857-2253.*

Tinkering on an airplane at the Kalamazoo Aviation History Museum

May-Sept.; fare), which explore sand hills and woods near Goshorn Lake on a larky 40-minute ride.

The town of **Holland** *(Visitors Bureau 616-392-2389 or 800-506-1299)* makes much of its Dutch antecedents, sparing no open ground a planting of tulips. Just a few blocks from the downtown area, you can see the big white arms of a 230-year-old windmill, still turning at **Windmill Island** *(Lincoln Ave. at 7th St. 616-355-1030. May-Oct.; adm. fee).* A drawbridge, gardens, farm animals, and an 1895 carousel are the main attractions, and more elements of an 18th-century Dutch community are under construction.

There is already a re-created 19th-century **Dutch Village** *(US 31 at James St. 616-396-1475. April-Oct.; adm. fee)* on Holland's north side. Miniaturized and commercial, it has canals winding among its brick shops, and *klompen* dancers in the summer. Wooden shoes such as the dancers wear—first used for work in the wet fields of France and the Netherlands—are made at the **DeKlomp Wooden Shoe and Delft Factory,** part of the **Veldheer Tulip Gardens** *(12755*

Dune buggy ride, Saugatuck

Quincy St. at US 31. 616-399-1900. April-Dec. daily, Jan.-March Mon.-Fri.; adm. fee to tulip gardens in spring). A sea of flowers erupts with colorful blossoms from May to October.

The route turns inland to **Grand Rapids** *(Visitors Bureau 616-459-8287 or 800-678-9859),* a sawmill center during Michigan's 19th-century timber boom, and home to the furniture factories that turned the felled forests into chairs and cabinets. Some of that historical handiwork is on display at the **Van Andel Museum Center** *(272 Pearl St. N.W. 616-456-3977. Adm. fee),* a spectacular new riverside building with exhibits that cover the area's history from the days when the Anishinabe people inhabited western Michigan. It keeps an eye on the present, too, using lasers and video to explore the night sky in the modern planetarium. For a taste of Grand Rapids' earlier heyday, visit the 1895 **Voigt House Victorian Museum** *(115 College Ave. S.E. 616-456-4600. Tues. and 2nd and 4th Sun.; adm. fee),* which contains the original furnishings and personal possessions of shop owner Carl G.A. Voigt and his family.

The nation's 38th President came from Grand Rapids, and his papers and memorabilia are found in the **Gerald R. Ford Museum** *(303 Pearl St. N.W. 616-451-9263. Adm. fee)*. The museum has a 20-minute video on Ford's career, and a full-scale reproduction of his Oval Office.

If the cool air of the Great Lakes makes you long for some tropical humidity, visit the **Frederick Meijer Gardens** *(3411 Bradford Ave. N.E. 616-957-1580. Adm. fee)*, 70 acres indoors and outdoors, with habitats ranging from tropical to desert. A varied collection of bronze sculptures are scattered throughout the nature trails and conservatories.

The Grand River moves west and so again does this route, arriving at the river's lake outlet at ❷ **Grand Haven** *(Visitors Bureau 616-842-4499 or 800-303-4096)*. This is where Grand Rapids families go in the summer, joined by other visitors who cruise into the harbor on pleasure boats. In Grand Haven and other lakeshore towns, you can hire a fishing rig and troll the big lake or the rivers that flow into it—check with local visitor bureaus for a list of fishing charters.

Some fine (and pricey) boats are on display during a stroll along the 2.5-mile **Grand Haven boardwalk ★**, which starts at the foot of the down-town area and follows the Grand River to Spring Lake. It leads to the South Pier and its lighthouse, and the sand beach at popular **Grand Haven State Park** *(1001 Harbor Ave. 616-798-3711)*. The walk is less peaceful at the height of the summer sea-son, when crowds gather along the boardwalk to see and hear

DeKlomp Wooden Shoe and Delft Factory, Holland

the "world's largest musical fountain," a mechanized out-pouring that springs and sings from the hillside across the harbor. The bleachers for fountain fans are behind the **Tri-Cities Historical Museum** *(1 N. Harbor St. 616-842-0700. Closed Mon.; adm. fee)*, a fine little repository with maritime and household artifacts of a century ago. Here you pick up tidbits of maritime lore—for instance, that "Ahoy" was the boarding cry of rampaging Vikings; and that "Mind your p's and q's" was not a schoolmarm's admonition, but a warning to sailors on shore leave to watch how many pints and quarts they quaffed.

If you want to learn something about the towering

sand dunes along this shore, or to hike around or up one, go north of town to **P.J. Hoffmaster State Park**★ *(6585 Lake Harbor Rd. 616-798-3573. Adm. fee),* where one massive dune has bellied up behind the E. Genevieve Gillette Visitor Center. Naturalists guide hikes through sand, forest, and marsh, explaining the continuous movement of these enormous sandy hills. Visitors can climb 160 steps to a spectacular view of the blue lake from atop a dune (don't roll down without permission—sand dunes are delicate creatures). There's a popular swimming beach here, too.

The route now follows the coast north to ❸ **Muskegon** *(Visitors Bureau 616-722-3751 or 800-235-3866).* Once a smoky industrial center known as the "Lumber Queen of the World," the town is now struggling to remake itself as a coastal resort. To do so, the city plays its historic hand, and the trump card is the 1890 **Hackley and Hume Historic Site**★ *(6th St. and Webster Ave. 616-722-7578. Mid-May–Sept. Wed. and Sat.-Sun.; adm. fee),* two elaborately ornamented Queen Anne houses with a shared carriage barn. The residences have been furnished and painted in the style of the 1880s lumber barons who built them. When he wasn't showing off his wealth in the house, Charles Hackley was a generous patron of the arts, and a founder of the **Muskegon Museum of Art** *(296 W. Webster Ave. 616-722-2600. Closed Mon.),* which retains an excellent collection of paintings. Permanent displays feature Rembrandt, Degas, Homer, and Whistler. John Stewart Curry's dramatic "Tornado Over Kansas" is in the large American collection.

Many historic boats have gone down in the Great Lakes, but the one tied up in Muskegon was *meant* to: the **USS *Silversides*** *(S side of Muskegon Channel Wall, at 1346 Bluff. 616-755-1230. Daily May-Sept., weekends April and Sept.-Oct.; adm. fee)* is a submarine that sank 23 enemy ships in the Pacific Theater during World War II. You can see how it worked, from propulsion to torpedoes, and visit the quarters in which the seamen—no claustrophobes, one hopes—lived.

Just north of town spreads 1,165-acre **Muskegon State Park** *(616-744-3480),* a piney reserve with miles of hiking trails and a scenic drive along the lakeshore.

Continue up the coast to **Whitehall,** where the next major river mouth opens into White Lake before emptying into Lake Michigan. Narrow, winding Murray Road rambles west along the lake's southern shore to the **White River Light Station Museum** *(616-894-8265.*

Fresnel lens, Tri-Cities Historical Museum, Grand Haven

Mem. Day–Labor Day Tues.-Sun., Sept. weekends; adm. fee), an octagonal brick lighthouse dating from 1875 with a small, interesting museum. A spiral staircase leads to a tower view of Lake Michigan, a Fresnel lens of the type used during the oil-burning days, plus photographs and artifacts that relate to maritime heritage.

Stairway to Lake Michigan, Muskegon State Park

93

Continue north along the lakeshore to **Silver Lake,** another example of lakes forming behind dunes that cut off or slow a river outlet into Lake Michigan. The dunes here are "live" ones, unanchored by trees or grass, and moving east 10 to 20 feet a year into Silver Lake, which still has plenty of room for swimming and boating. An area of dunes at the north end of ➍ **Silver Lake State Park** *(16th Ave., Mears. 616-873-3083)* is open to off-road vehicles *(permit required),* but your best bet is to take a passenger seat on **Mac Woods' Dune Rides** *(629 N. 18th Ave. 616-873-2817. Mid-May–mid-Oct.; fare),* which operate in the park's south end. Drivers zoom open-air, fat-tire vehicles up and down the sand with guide commentary. Between these two motorized areas is a long stretch of quiet beach, where you can stroll on sculptured sand or catch a rosy sunset.

Much of the lakeshore is private land studded with state parks. Inland to the east, though, sprawls 964,711-acre **Huron-Manistee National Forests**★ *(Huron-Manistee Ranger Station 616-723-2211 or 800-821-6263),* a patchwork of federal forestlands with some fine stretches of river, marshes, and primitive areas closed to vehicles. The easygoing rivers are popular with canoeists, kayakers, and rafters. Going from south to north, the White River upstream from Whitehall is the first popular float; then comes the Pere Marquette, meandering through tall forest; the Big Sable River flows into Hamlin Lake; and, finally, the Little Manistee and the Manistee Rivers arrive

at Lake Michigan at their namesake town. The rivers are no challenge to paddlers, but the thick forest, good fishing for steelhead, trout, and walleye, and views of wildlife such as deer, river otters, and eagles, make them appealing.

Managed under the elusive concept of multiple use, the forest has opened special areas to mountain biking, off-road vehicles, snowmobiles, and cross-country skiing. The **North Country National Scenic Trail,** which connects upstate New York with North Dakota, runs through the forest on its way from Grand Rapids to the Upper Peninsula.

Just south of Ludington, **White Pine Village** *(1587 S. Lakeshore Dr. 616-843-4808. Mem. Day–Labor Day Tues.-Sun.; adm. fee)* is a collection of historical buildings—including a blacksmith shop, hardware store, and logging and maritime museum—centered around an 1850s county courthouse. North of town lies **Ludington State Park** *(End of Mich. 116. 616-843-8671),* with one

Ludington City Lighthouse

of the state's longest, most popular beaches. If you tire of lying on the sand, there are 18 miles of trails over dunes and through forests, Hamlin Lake for swimming and boating, and a Visitor Center with displays and a video on the Great Lakes. It's a 1.5-mile hike north of the park to the **Point Sable Lighthouse** *(616-845-7343. Closed Wed.-Thurs.),* an 1866 tower now cased in black-and-white steel cladding.

Hikers can continue dune-tramping north into **Nordhouse Dunes Wilderness Area** *(Forest Trail Rd. 616-723-2211),* part of Manistee National Forest. It's only 3,450 acres, but its primitive quality seems to discourage visitors. This is a good wildflower site in the spring, and there are oddly shaped fungi growing in its marshy pine woods interior; also, a lovely, lonely beach. You can pitch your tent where you wish, but if you want a managed campground, look for the **Lake Michigan Recreation**

Area *(Forest Trail Rd. 616-723-6716)* on the north edge of the wilderness.

❺ Manistee *(Chamber of Commerce 616-723-2575 or 800-288-2286)* grew as a lumber town around the mouth of the Little Manistee River. The **Manistee County Historical Museum** *(425 River St. 616-723-5531. June-Sept. Mon.-Sat., Tues.-Sat. rest of year; adm. fee)* maintains the Lyman Drug Store as it was in the 1880s, with apothecary scales and mysterious powders and potions; other rooms re-create a newspaper office, a dentist's workplace, and a general store.

The many small pleasures of the coastline are writ large at **❻ Sleeping Bear Dunes National Lakeshore**★★ *(9922 Front St., Empire. 616-326-5134. Adm. fee),* where the wonder of ever-changing dunes, shipwrecks, and North Woods wilderness take on a monumental scale. The protected shoreline stretches 35 miles. From the dune ridges, visitors can scan layered dunes, high bluffs, rivers, and forests, as well as the big blue bowl of Lake Michigan.

Chippewa legend has it that the lakeshore's namesake dune, on a bluff reaching out into Manitou Passage, is a sleeping bear, and the two offshore islands, South and North Manitou, are cubs that drowned trying to reach her. She is one big bruin, but not as big as she used to be. During the past century, parts of the bluff have collapsed into the lake, and the particles of windblown sand that sometimes sting faces are part of an endless reshaping process.

The park has 13 trails, including the **Empire Bluff Trail,** which visits maple forest and dune peaks on an easy 2-mile hike. Drive along **Pierce Stocking Scenic Drive** *(Off Mich. 109. April–mid-Nov.),* a 7.1-mile auto loop that offers views of the dunes north and south. Tackling the steep, 150-foot **Dune Climb,** surrounded by pastel sand and the blue wash of sky, huffing hikers feel like they've stepped into a Georgia O'Keeffe painting.

The Manitou Passage is a shortcut for hurried freighters that has proven fatal for many ships (see sidebar this page), and the crews at the Coast Guard station on Sleeping Bear Point trained rigorously for rescues. Videos and displays at the **Sleeping Bear Point Coast Guard Station Maritime Museum** *(1 mile W of Glen Haven. 616-334-3225. Mem. Day–Labor Day)* show the drills of the crew and describe some of the wrecks. Lifeboats and fishing gear are displayed at the nearby **Glen Haven Cannery.**

Just north of the national lakeshore lies the town of **Leland** *(Chamber of Commerce 616-256-9895),* whose early history—replete with settlers and shipwrecks—is well

Shipwrecks

Lake Michigan has had more than its share of maritime disasters—more major wrecks, in fact, than the other Great Lakes combined. Among the most fateful ship graveyards is the Manitou Passage, long a tempting shortcut for ships on their way up or down Lake Michigan. At least 50 ships have gone down here, the most recent being the *Francisco Morazan,* which ran aground off South Manitou Island in 1960 with a load of chickens, lard, and machinery. As sands shift, "new" wrecks are discovered now and then. In 1996 the lumber steamer *Three Brothers* was discovered 85 years after it went down. The state has created the Manitou Passage State Underwater Preserve, one of nine areas around the state set up to protect shipwrecks. For more information contact the Michigan Underwater Preserve Council, Inc. *(560 N. State St., St. Ignace, MI 49781).* Divers who disturb or remove artifacts can be jailed and fined.

told at the **Leelanau Historical Museum** *(203 E. Cedar St. 616-256-7475. Mem. Day–Labor Day Tues.-Sun., Fri.-Sat. rest of year; adm. fee).* But the main reason people come here is to stop by the weatherbeaten row of stilted shanties along the harbor called **Fishtown.** Fishermen air their nets and sportfishing outfitters pick up passengers, while the shacks house art galleries and souvenir and snack shops.

Here, too, you can hop a ferry *(Manitou Island Transit 616-256-9061. June-Aug. daily, call for May and Sept.-Oct. schedule; fare)* to **North** and **South Manitou Islands,** part of the national lakeshore. A century ago, these islands were home to self-sufficient farmers, who raised peas, cherries, and prizewinning rye; only a few ruins remain from that time. If you stop at North Manitou *(ferries run July–Labor Day Wed. and Fri.-Mon. only)* to hike its 30 miles of trails, be prepared to camp overnight in bare-bones style—the ferry makes only one visit a day. At South Manitou you can take a historic tour *(arrange through Manitou Island Transit),* visit the world's tallest white cedar in the Valley of the Giants, follow a ranger through the 104-foot lighthouse, and return the same day.

The peninsula north of Leland is called Michigan's "little finger," with a beckoning eastward bend that encloses Grand Traverse Bay. **Leelanau State Park** *(Cty. Rd. 629. 616-386-5422. Adm. fee)* has a white fingernail of secluded beach along Cathead Bay, and a rustic campground at the northernmost point of land where stands the **Grand Traverse Lighthouse** *(Open summer).* The 1916 lighthouse contains a maritime museum, and you can climb to the widow's walk around its octagonal light.

The route now follows the west shore of Grand Traverse Bay south, with a nice view of the West Arm, to
❼ Traverse City *(Visitors Bureau 616-947-5075 or 800-872-8377).* Lumber fortunes built the city, but today it's tourism, fishing, and fruit—particularly grapes and cherries—that keep it bustling. Replacing the schooners that once swept in and out with loads of pine planks is the **Tall Ship *Malabar*★** *(13390 S. West Bay Shore Dr. 616-941-2000. May-Sept.; fare),* a two-masted schooner that sets sail with a cargo of tourists several times a day. Guests can also spend the night on board.

The music at the **Interlochen Center for the Arts**★ *(Mich. 137, across from Interlochen State Park. 616-276-6230)* is well worth a 15-mile detour south of town. Students and renowned guests—comedian Bill Cosby and cellist Yo-Yo Ma in the past—frequently perform music, theater,

---

Fine Wines

Gourmet wine country? The Great Lakes? Maybe a sunburnt afternoon getting zonked at an island vineyard in Lake Erie. Fun wine, not fine. But a taste of Merlot from Château Chantal on the Old Mission Peninsula could shift opinion. And the nearby Château Grand Traverse's Johannisberg Riesling has proved that prize-winning dry Vinifera grapes can survive the Michigan winters. A second winegrowing area in southwest Michigan has had similar success, with such wine labels as Lemon Creek, Tabor Hill, and St. Julian. But let's face it. This is neither Burgundy, nor Napa. For the moment, Michigan growers concentrate on their regional market, and vintners such as Robert Begin make converts with a sip or two on a quiet evening in Château Chantal's **Great Room** *(616-223-4110),* overlooking Traverse Bay.

and dance shows, and exhibit visual art.

Another kind of ferment is going on along the **Old Mission Peninsula ★**, a thin stick of land that bisects Grand Traverse Bay, pointing north. Temperatures on the peninsula, accessible via Mich. 37, are moderated by the lake, making it a strong competitor in Michigan's expanding community of vintners. **Château Grand Traverse** *(12239 Center Rd. 616-223-7355. April-Oct. daily, Nov.-March Sun.-Fri.)* has been winning prizes for 20 years. Lately it's been joined by the **Château Chantal Winery ★** *(15900 Rue de Vin. 616-223-4110)*, which also rents rooms in its magnificent ridgetop winery, with watery views on either side. If you have not yet had your fill of lighthouses, follow the call of gulls to **Lighthouse Park** *(End of Mich. 37)*, with a small, peaceful beach.

The route rambles north on US 31 to **Charlevoix** *(Chamber of Commerce 616-547-2101)*, a resort town that has succeeded beyond its own dreams, and, perhaps, capacity. Amid much new building on both Lake Michigan and Lake Charlevoix stand some intriguing houses built 50 years ago by developer Earl Young, with curving, shingled roofs and local stone. For a look at lifestyles of the rich and not-necessarily-famous, walk along the inlet to Round Lake (from Bridge Street to Michigan Avenue) and exclaim over the luxury yachts.

Still farther north awaits

❽ Petoskey *(Visitors Bureau 616-347-4150)*, another old resort town with the reek of

97

Sleeping Bear Dunes National Lakeshore

new money. Shoppers and diners crowd into the historical **Gaslight District** *(Bordered by Mitchell, Bay, Howard, and Lake Sts.)*. Young Ernest Hemingway often summered up this way, and so earns a place in the **Little Traverse Historical Museum** *(1 Waterfront Pk. 616-347-2620. May-Oct. Tues.-Sat.; donation)*. Housed in an 1892 turreted railroad depot, the museum has exhibits on regional settlement, historic crafts of the Odawa Indians, and materials of writer Bruce Catton, who was born in town in 1899.

Upper Peninsula ★★

● **450 miles** ● **3 to 5 days** ● **May to Oct.**

In the early 19th century, when the Northwest Territory was divvied up into new states, the chunk of densely forested, wind-whipped land sticking out into the lakes east of Wisconsin was not exactly the top prize. The real estate that Michigan politicos sought was a valuable port to the south, along Lake Erie...but that went to Ohio. Michigan had to settle for the Upper Peninsula: an impenetrable, weatherbeaten wilderness of little apparent value. As you journey through this remarkable landscape 170 years later, ask yourself: "Would I rather be in Toledo?" Sorry, Ohio, but you know the answer.

A world apart from lower Michigan's outstretched "mitten," the Upper Peninsula is a land of higher latitudes and lower temperatures, waterfalls and fallen forests, snowpacks and wolf packs. It is defined by the lakes that surround it, particularly Lake Superior, the icy cauldron that holds one-tenth of the world's fresh water, and the hulls of many ships that went down in its storms.

Beginning in the port of Sault Ste. Marie, this tour moves west to explore Whitefish Bay, Pictured Rocks National Lakeshore, and other wonders on the rugged Lake Superior shore, as well as nearby wildlands. Farther west, the drive pauses at the historic shipping port of Marquette, before veering south through Hiawatha National Forest. Assorted coastal sights punctuate the route as it loops east to St. Ignace, jumping-off point for the last stop, Mackinac Island.

Lake Superior is so vast that ships in the distance may not look like much…but at ❶ **Sault Ste. Marie** *(Visitors Bureau 906-632-3301 or 800-647-2858)* you can see close up the incredible length and girth of today's freighters as they squeeze through a series of locks down into Lake Huron. The Indians and French voyageurs once portaged around this stretch of the St. Marys River, where it tumbles down a slope from Lake Superior to Lake Huron, a 21-foot drop. It was the discovery of iron deposits in the west, and the need to ship the ore east, that compelled the state of Michigan to install the first series of major locks in 1855.

A pleasant strip of shady park buffers the huge locks of the U.S. Army Corps of Engineers from downtown Sault Ste. Marie. At the Corps' **Soo Locks Visitors Center**★★ *(W. Portage Ave. 906-632-2394. Mid-May–mid-Nov., locks usually operate mid-March–Dec.)*, onlookers tour historical exhibits explaining how locks work, then watch from an observation deck as the big ships—some nearly as long as the Empire State Building is tall—maneuver through MacArthur Lock. Signs in the center tell you when ships are expected.

Like every maritime museum within spitting distance of the lake, this one has an exhibit on the 1975 wreck of the *Edmund Fitzgerald.*

A couple of blocks from the river stands the hulking **Tower of History** *(326 E. Portage Ave. 906-632-3658. Mid-May–mid-Oct.; adm. fee)*, which has threadbare displays but offers a great view of the locks from its 21-story height.

Sailing on Lake Huron

Maritime history is more gripping at the **Museum Ship Valley Camp**★ *(Johnston and Water Sts. 906-632-3658. Mid-May–mid-Oct.; adm. fee)*, a retired 550-foot freighter. Here you'll find more extensive exhibits, including ship models, a ship's helm so big it took four men to turn, and lifeboats from the ill-fated *Edmund Fitzgerald.* From docks nearby you can board **Soo Locks Boat Tours and Dinner Cruises** *(515 and 1157 E. Portage Ave. 906-632-6301. Mid-May–mid-Oct.; fare)*, for a two-hour cruise that offers a lift through the locks and a close look at passing freighters.

From Sault Ste. Marie, go south on I-75, west on Mich. 28, and north on Mich. 221 to Brimley; here, pick up Lake Shore Drive and move west, along Lake Superior's Whitefish Bay. Tunneling through white birches, maples, and oaks, you pass **Point Iroquois Light Station** *(Lake Shore Dr. 906-437-5272. Mid-May–mid-Oct.; donation),* where you can climb to the top of the 65-foot tower to view the headwaters of the St. Marys River; **Pendills Creek National Fish Hatchery** *(Lake Shore Dr. 906-437-5231. Mon.-Fri.),* where lake trout are raised to restock the Great Lakes; and long views of turquoise waters and sandy beaches.

Take Mich. 123 north to Paradise and continue north to Whitefish Point. This spit of land, jutting into waters so treacherous they have been dubbed the "Graveyard of the Great Lakes," is an apt location for the **Whitefish Point Lighthouse & Great Lakes Shipwreck Historical Museum** ★★ *(110 Whitefish Pt. Rd. 906-635-1742. Mid-May–mid-Oct.; adm. fee).* Before a light was erected here in 1848, accidents were so frequent that newspaper editor Horace Greeley wrote, "Every month's delay is a virtual manslaughter." The current skeleton-framed light dates back to 1861. It overlooks a gentle sand beach, a nice place to unwind after a visit to the fascinating, but sometimes grim, museum, with its litany of wrecks and deaths from the earliest schooners to the inevitable *Edmund Fitzgerald* exhibit (an excellent video describes the salvaging of the *Fitzgerald*).

Memorial to lost sailors, Whitefish Point

Across the parking lot from the museum sprawls the **Whitefish Point Bird Observatory** ★ *(906-492-3596. April–mid-Oct.),* the first spit of land that birds can touch down on when crossing the lake heading south, and a gathering place before they jump north. Hawks, loons, ducks, and geese are among the many kinds that show up, particularly in April, May, October, and November. There is an information center and an observation station.

To explore the Upper Peninsula's wealth of undeveloped wildlands, the route backtracks down Whitefish Point Road and heads west on Mich. 123 to 40,000-acre ❷ **Tahquamenon Falls State Park** *(Mich. 123. 906-492-3415. Adm. fee).* Spilling over two falls within the park, the Tahquamenon River appears rusty brown—caused by tannin leached from cedar, spruce, and hemlock in swamps farther upstream. Most people take the easy hike from the concessionaire to the Lower Falls; you can also rent a boat from the concessionaire and row to the falls. The Upper Falls are accessible by a longer, more difficult trail; or visit them aboard an enjoyable day-long trolley-riverboat cruise from Soo Junction *(Toonerville Trolley and Boat Trips 906-876-2311. June-Oct.; fare).*

The route proceeds southwest on Mich. 123 and Mich. 28 to Seney. Here, wildlife lovers will want to detour south to the **Seney National Wildlife Refuge** *(Mich. 77. 906-586-9851. Visitor Center open mid-May–mid-Oct.).* The 95,000-acre refuge encloses the Great Manistique Swamp—marshy tamarack woods roamed by moose, wolves, black bears, and muskrat. Humans can roam by foot or bicycle, or canoe the Manistique River. The 7-mile round-trip **Marshland Wildlife Drive** offers great eagle- and loon-watching.

Mich. 77 winds north to **Grand Marais,** a cozy harbor town with easy access to the adjacent ❸ **Pictured Rocks National Lakeshore** ★★ *(906-387-3700).* One of the most alluring stretches of coastline on the

Storm clouds over Whitefish Bay

Great Lakes, the 200-foot limestone cliffs were chiseled by powerful winds, waves, and ice into arches, knobs, and terraces; then minerals painted them oranges, rusts, and reds. Those who want the extraordinary offshore view of the rocks can take a 3-hour boat cruise *(Pictured Rocks Boat Cruises, Municipal Pier, Munising. 906-387-2379. Mem. Day–mid-Oct.; fare)* past Miners Castle, Caves of Bloody Chiefs, Battleship Rock, and other rock formations. You can also fly along the cliffs *(Skylane, Hanley Landing Field, Munising. 906-222-8367. Mem. Day–mid-Oct.; adm. fee)* for a bird's-eye view. There is much to do on land as well, including fishing, swimming, and hiking.

At the lakeshore's **Grand Sable Visitor Center** *(Cty. Rd. H58, just W of Grand Marais. 906-494-2660. Mid-May–mid-Oct.),* you can get information on other sights, including **Sable Falls** and the 1874 **Au Sable Point Light Station** *(1.5-mile hike beyond Hurricane River Campground. 906-494-2660. Tours May-Aug. Tues.-Sat.)*. The 43-mile Lakeshore Trail follows the lakeshore west, or take a rough, unpaved inland road (Cty. Rd. 53) that brings you to trailheads near the beach.

Chapel Falls, Pictured Rocks National Lakeshore

Off the shores of Munising abruptly rises a big chunk of forested rock— **Grand Island**★, a national recreation area managed by **Hiawatha National Forest** *(906-387-3700)*. Visitors can take a ferry over *(Grand Island Landing, Mich. 28. 906-387-3503. Mem. Day–mid-Oct.; fare)* to Grand Island and join a tour that covers the island's sights and history. Scuba divers love the Grand Island area for its shipwrecks, as well as underwater caves. Ships such as the three-masted *Granada* are sunk in fairly shallow water; you can see them via glass-bottom boats with **Grand Island Shipwreck Tours** *(1204 Commercial St., Munising. 906-387-4477. June-Sept.; fare)*. In deeper waters, there are many more wrecks, some still intact a century after going down. The state protects them from vandals (see sidebar page 95) and marks them with buoys as part of the **Alger Underwater Preserve**★.

The tour follows the coast west on Mich. 28 to **④ Marquette** *(Visitors Bureau 906-228-7749 or 800-544-4321)*, the main shipping port for the iron ore that has been the lifeblood of the Upper Peninsula economy since the middle 19th century. Huge lakers still load ore several times a week. The enormous wealth carved from the Upper Peninsula's three iron ranges paid for some fine buildings, including century-old mansions on the bluffs with a view of Presque Isle Point to the north. Guided and self-guided walking tours of Marquette's historic districts are available at the **Marquette County Historical Museum** *(213 N. Front St. 906-226-3571. Mon.-Fri.; adm. fee)*, which also has exhibits on mining and Chippewa culture.

For the full story of iron in the Upper Peninsula, take a detour 8 miles west to the **Michigan Iron Industry Museum**★ *(73 Forge Rd. 906-475-7857. May-Oct.)*, which occupies the site of an iron forge built in the 1840s, shortly after the first big veins were discovered. The life of hardworking immigrant miners comes back vividly in videos and exhibits.

Now the route winds south on US 41 and east on US 2 through the western unit of **Hiawatha National Forest** *(906-786-4062),* where the woods have regrown since the big clearcuts of the 1930s. Deer and black bears, trout and bass, songbirds and ducks make this a wildlife paradise, and a favorite of hunters and fishermen. At the forest's southern end, the **Garden Peninsula** extends 21 miles into Lake Michigan. This is farm country that has also felt the bite of the miner's shovel. The Jackson Iron Company built a smelter in ❺ **Fayette,** with houses for its workers, and an opera house. After the smelter shutdown it was a ghost town for 70 years before the state restored the buildings as part of **Historic Fayette Townsite ★,** located in **Fayette State Park** *(Mich. 183. 906-644-2603. Mid-May–mid-Oct.; adm. fee).* A self-guided walking tour provides insight into the preserved industrial community.

If you haven't yet lost your appetite for lighthouses, you'll enjoy stopping by the **Seul Choix Point Lighthouse** *(Cty. Rd. 432, S of Gulliver. 906-283-3183. June-Sept.; adm. fee),* built in 1895. It has a small but growing museum in the light keeper's quarters, and you can climb the 78-foot tower.

At the Upper Peninsula's southeasternmost tip, you reach a finger of land pointing toward the spot where Lake Michigan flows into Lake Huron—the Straits of Mackinac. This juncture has been a fulcrum of historic

events, with Indians, French, British, and Americans all vying for control of these waters. Among the first in the area, the well-traveled missionary Jacques Marquette founded the town of **St. Ignace** *(Chamber of Commerce 906-643-8717 or 800-338-6660)* in 1671. His burial spot is marked next to **Marquette Mission Park and Museum of Ojibwa Culture ★** *(500-566 N. State St. 906-643-9161. Mem. Day–Oct.; adm. fee),* where

Historic Fayette Townsite

exhibits focus on the Ojibwe, the original inhabitants of the upper Great Lakes region. Visitors can learn about their view of the cosmos and read the translations of tribal histories that were recorded on birchbark scrolls. Outside, a Huron longhouse and Victorian-style garden

Lighthouse B&Bs

High-tech navigation methods have almost made lighthouses obsolete. The lights that once warned ships away from shoals now lure tourists—and a few are even offering overnight stays. At the 1869 **Big Bay Lighthouse Bed and Breakfast** *(Big Bay, follow signs from Cty. Rd. 550. 906-345-9957),* the antique-furnished rooms in the redbrick light keeper's house are attached to the light tower. You can climb a spiral staircase to an open platform that surrounds the light, which still flashes. The **Sand Hills Lighthouse Inn** *(Five Mile Point Rd., W of Marquette. 906-337-1744)* rests on a point on the Keweenaw Peninsula. If you find you'll be arriving late, there's no need to ask the owners to "leave the light on."

are maintained. Tribal members are sometimes found beading or making baskets in the back of the museum.

More can be learned about the peripatetic Frenchman at the **Father Marquette National Memorial and Museum** *(Straits State Park, 720 Church St. 906-643-9394. Mid-May–Sept.; adm. fee)*, located on the bluffs west of St. Ignace. The park also has interpretive walks.

Right next to the park, the **Mackinac Bridge** *(Toll)* forms a 5-mile arc to the Lower Peninsula. The towers of "Mighty Mac" rise 552 feet above the straits, and on windy days the bridge bows as much as 20 feet sideways.

On the Lower Peninsula side of the bridge lies
6 **Mackinaw City,** which seemed a perfect site for a fur-trading outpost in 1715 when French soldiers built Fort Michilimackinac—now **Colonial Michilimackinac ★** *(Off I-75, just S of bridge. 616-436-5563. Mid-May–mid-Oct.; adm. fee)*, a national historic landmark. The British took over the fort in 1760, withstood a beating from Chief Pontiac and the Ojibwe in 1763, and later moved their garrison to Mackinac Island. After extensive archaeological research (you can enter a tunnel dig and view newly discovered artifacts), the fort has been rebuilt. Interpreters dress as redcoats and French traders, and a colonial wedding dance is periodically reenacted.

Colonial Michilimackinac is operated by Mackinac Associates, a nonprofit group that also manages Mackinac Island State Park and Fort Mackinac. They have a fourth site as well, **Historic Mill Creek State Historic Park ★** *(US 23, E of Mackinaw City. 616-436-7301. Mid-May–mid-Oct.; adm. fee)*, an 18th-century water-powered sawmill.

Ferries from Mackinaw City *(ferry information 616-436-5542. Fare)* and St. Ignace *(ferry information 906-847-3351. Fare)* ply thousands of visitors annually to **7** **Mackinac Island ★ ★** *(616-436-5563. Visitor Center, Huron St. across from Marquette Park. 906-847-1000. State park open year-round, Fort Mackinac open May–mid-Oct., other historic sites open May–Labor Day, Grand Hotel open mid-May–Oct.)*. One day is not nearly enough time to explore the historic sites, restaurants, and natural beauty of this 3-mile-long island—most of which is a state park. There are no cars…and the lake air seems fresher, the pace more relaxed than on the mainland. The 8.2-mile trek around the island's perimeter on Lake Shore Road can be made by foot, horseback *(906-847-3573)*, carriage *(906-847-3573)*, or bicycle. Whatever mode of transport you choose, be sure to venture up to **Sugar Loaf** or **Arch Rock,** where you'll be rewarded with fine views.

Hardy Party

When the ferries unload at Mackinac Island on an August weekend, it sometimes looks as if the New York Marathon was rerouted. Yet there was a time when the crowds here were even larger. In the 1820s the island was the heart of John Jacob Astor's fur-trade empire, as well as a military outpost. Thousands of beaver pelts (gathered from the Northwest Territory) were dried, cleaned, graded, sorted, and shipped at Mackinac. As many as 3,000 Indians would camp on the beach, and thousands of woodsmen, clerks, and voyageurs would live in tents, barracks, or on open ground. There were also soldiers garrisoned at the fort to make sure the British didn't try to sneak back over through the straits. These days, Mackinac is quite a party town on a warm summer night. But today's festivities can't top those of years ago—in the early 19th century a frontiersman back from a long stay in the wilderness was naturally deserving of an all-night celebration!

In addition to a surfeit of gift, candy, and snack shops, the downtown area boasts several restored historical buildings, particularly along **Market Street.** Don't miss the scary tools in the **Benjamin Blacksmith Shop**★ *(May–Labor Day; adm. free with Fort Mackinac ticket).*

The grass of Marquette Park slopes up to Fort Mackinac and its white ramparts, above the town. If you're walking up, you might stop first at the 1838 **Indian**

Grand Hotel, Mackinac Island

Dormitory *(Huron St. Adm. free with Fort Mackinac ticket)* and view displays on the culture of the island's former Native American residents. An 18th-century British outpost, **Fort Mackinac**★★ *(906-847-3328. May–mid-Oct.; adm. fee)* was later awarded to America through treaties. The fort is preserved as a museum, with a restored commissary, barracks, and quarters, among other buildings. Interpreters dressed as soldiers (American, not British) blow their horns and discharge their muskets. Visitors can soak up a view of the straits by taking tea at the Officers' Tea Room.

Bring some proper clothes if you'd rather sip your tea at the 1887 **Grand Hotel**★ *(1 Grand Ave. 906-847-3331. May–mid-Oct.).* Perched on the island's west side, it has a wonderful sunset view from its 660-foot veranda (if you're not a guest, it's pay-per-view). You can, of course, get a similar view—in less formal garb—from the rocky beaches along the lakeshore.

Back on the mainland, I-75 north leads back to Sault Ste. Marie.

Coastal Loop★★

● 400 miles ● 4 to 5 days ● Spring through autumn

The Door Peninsula extends into Lake Michigan like a finger held to the wind, something the fishermen of its coastal villages have been doing for centuries. Shielding Green Bay to the west, it now lures to its quaint towns visitors who see it as a Great Lakes version of New England. The charm was hard earned: The peninsula's name stems from Porte des Morts ("death's door"), which the French dubbed the channel between the peninsula's tip and Washington Island. It was known for its dangerous undercurrent even before the first of many sailing ships wrecked on its straits.

This loop travels from the outskirts of Milwaukee (see Milwaukee to the Dells drive, p. 114) up Wisconsin's east coast to the tip of the Door Peninsula and its off-lying islands. It continues to Green Bay, a city whose name can hardly be spoken without appending "Packers." Curving around Lake Winnebago through Oshkosh and Fond du

Lac, the tour finishes with a drive through Kettle Moraine State Forest.

Though only 10 miles north of the Milwaukee suburbs, the compact harbor at **❶ Port Washington**★ *(Chamber of Commerce 414-284-0900 or 800-719-4881)* has the feel of a small fishing village. Despite the looming power-plant smokestacks above the shaded breakwater, it's the sight of fishermen casting peacefully from the rocks below that sets the tone. Once a commercial fishing port, this is now a favorite spot for sportfishing *(call chamber for list of charters)*. If you don't catch your own, the venerable **Smith Bros. Fish Shanty Restaurant and Market** *(100 N. Franklin St. 414-284-5592)* serves perch and walleye dishes, and beer from its own microbrewery. The **Captain's Quarters** *(219 N. Franklin St. 414-284-6789)*, a longtime sailor's bar with old photographs of the port, has a dance floor like a ship's deck.

Beachcombers will hurry up the coast to the dunes sandwiched between Lake Michigan and the Black River at **Kohler-Andrae State Park**★ *(I-43 to Cty. Rd. V east, then right on Cty. Rd. KK to 1520 Old Park Rd. 920-451-4080. Adm. fee)*. Outside the **Sanderling Nature Center** *(Daily June-Aug., weekends May and Sept.-Oct.)* lies the keel of an 1850s schooner, a testimony to the many shipwrecks in the area. Inside you can learn about the birds and rare plants in the wetlands before setting out for a walk on one of the nature trails or the beach. Boardwalks allow you to explore without disturbing the delicate dune flora.

Rogers Street Fishing Village, Two Rivers

Farther north lies the town of **Sheboygan** *(Chamber of Commerce 920-457-9491)*, settled by German immigrants in the 1840s—it's still known for its bratwurst. Old fishing shanties along the boardwalk where the Sheboygan River meets the harbor have been joined by art galleries and restaurants. The Kohler family founded a plumbing fixture empire here over a century ago. The **John Michael Kohler Arts Center**★ *(608 New York Ave. 920-458-6144)*, formerly the Kohler mansion, is a handsome old building of pale brick and wrought iron. The center exhibits contemporary art in five exhibition halls. Plumbing becomes an art form in three levels of

Coastal Loop

Ice Age Trail

Glaciers leave gigantic footprints—you can see the outline of their paths in the moraines and kettles (ridges and potholes) that mark much of the Great Lakes landscape. More than 10,000 years ago, sheets of mile-thick ice blanketed about two-thirds of Wisconsin. The 1,000-mile **Ice Age National Scenic Trail** (414-691-2776) winds across the state—from Potawatomi State Park on Sturgeon Bay to Interstate State Park on the St. Croix River. About 600 miles of the trail are open to the public, with more links added every year. For further information on the ridges and rounded hills left in the glacier's wake, visit the **Henry S. Reuss Ice Age Visitor Center** (Wis. 67, near Dundee. 920-533-8322).

display at the **Kohler Design Center**★ (101 Upper Rd. 920-457-3699. Factory tours Mon.-Fri.), featuring the company's own "great wall of china." Factory tours visit the kilns and iron foundry. For a change of pace, take the self-guided walking tour at **Indian Mound Park** (Panther Ave. and S. 9th St. 920-459-3444) among 18 effigy mounds in the forms of birds, deer, and geometric shapes, made by Woodland Indians around A.D. 500.

Farther north, ❷ **Manitowoc** (Chamber of Commerce 920-684-5575) grew from a succession of lake port industries—lumber, fishing, and boatbuilding. After producing top-of-the-line schooners in the 19th century, the shipyards turned out submarines during World War II. The USS *Cobia*, moored at the **Wisconsin Maritime Museum**★ (75 Maritime Dr. 920-684-0218. Adm. fee), recounts a century of shipping on the Great Lakes with displays of hand-crafted ship models and historical photographs.

Just north of Manitowoc on Wis. 42 sprawls **Two Rivers,** a busy sport- and commercial fishing port. The townpeople's French-Canadian predecessors are memorialized at the **Rogers Street Fishing Village** (2116 Jackson St. 920-793-5905. May-Oct.; adm. fee) with a fishing tug, shipwreck detritus, and the 1883 North Pier Lighthouse. Two Rivers claims to be the birthplace of the ice-cream sundae: The local historical society serves the original version at Berners' Ice Cream Parlor, part of the museum in the 1850 **Washington House** (1622 Jefferson St. 920-793-2490), which also serves as a hotel.

Continue north on Wis. 42 along the narrowing peninsula to Sturgeon Bay, where an isthmus connecting the lake to Green Bay became a shipping shortcut with the construction of a canal in 1878. **Sturgeon Bay** (Information Center 920-743-3924) has managed to fashion itself into an attractive resort town while continuing a tradition of ship- and yacht-building that began in 1836. The **Door County Maritime Museum**★ (120 N. Madison St. 920-743-5958. Adm. fee) has three quite different parts, spread around the peninsula. The Sturgeon Bay facility focuses on shipbuilding, and there's also a branch at the Cana Island Lighthouse, on the peninsula's east coast. Yet a third offshoot, at Gills Rock (12724 Wisconsin Bay Rd. 920-743-5958. Mem. Day–mid-Oct.; adm. fee), on the peninsula's northern tip, highlights the fishing industry.

Drive north on Wis. 57; in May, and you'll see cherry blossoms everywhere—up to 20 million pounds of cherries are harvested in Door County annually. A beach respite awaits at ❸ **Whitefish Dunes State Park**

(3700 Clark Lake Rd., near Sturgeon Bay. 920-823-2400. Adm. fee), which is recommended more for sunbathing than for swimming in cold Lake Michigan. The 13 miles of hiking trails avoid the easily eroded 90-foot dunes, but the views are beautiful, particularly going north on the White Trail above the rugged cliffs around Cave Point.

The breezy marina at **Baileys Harbor** is another nice walking area, and a launching point for sportfishermen. Just north of town on Wis. 57 and east on County Road Q, lies the **Ridges Sanctuary**★ *(8288 Cty. Rd. Q. 920-839-2802. Nature center open mid-May–mid-Oct., summer naturalist tours; adm. fee)*. Lake Michigan was once much larger than it is today, and the receding lake-shore left a series of ridges rich in flora and fauna, now protected at the 1,000-acre sanctuary. Trails run along the ridges; bridges cross the boggy swales in between. Lists of wildflowers in bloom are posted at the nature center—look for the many varieties of orchids.

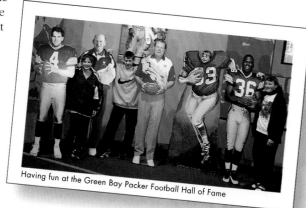

Having fun at the Green Bay Packer Football Hall of Fame

Continue north on County Road Q and Cana Island Road, to **Cana Island Lighthouse**★ *(920-743-5958. Grounds open year-round, call for lighthouse hours; adm. fee)*. You may have to take off your shoes and socks to wade across the causeway to Cana Island (depending on weather and season), but it's worth it. The 1869 lighthouse rises on its small, forested island like a shrine, with a minaret-shaped peak on top. Keepers sometimes show visitors inside.

At the peninsula's end, take the car ferry from North-port *(Washington Island Ferry Line 920-847-2546. Fare)* to ❹ **Washington Island**★ *(Chamber of Commerce 920-847-2179)*, a quiet community of resorts and marinas. The ferry crosses the swift currents of Porte des Morts, a treacherous strait where conditions can change very fast. Legend has it that in 1914 the mail crossed by motorboat in the morning and a car drove back over the ice that night. From Detroit Harbor, drive, taxi, or bicycle around the island to Jackson Harbor where you can catch another ferry *(Rock Island Ferry 920-847-2252. Mem. Day–Columbus Day, or by appt.; fare)* to **Rock Island State Park★★.** The island is a peaceable kingdom (no cars allowed) once owned by an inventor-millionaire, Chester Thordarson, who built various stone buildings to honor his Icelandic roots. Among them is the high-ceilinged Viking Hall boathouse, now home to the park's nature center *(920-847-2235. Mem. Day–Columbus Day)*.

After ferrying back to the peninsula, head south on Wis. 42 along the west shore. You'll pass through a series of picturesque villages—Ellison Bay, Sister Bay, Ephraim, and Egg Harbor—most with curio and antique shops, and restaurants where you might see a sign for a "Fish Boil." There are also roadside fruit stands selling apples and cherries, and some orchards where you can do your own picking. Between Ephraim and Fish Creek awaits **Peninsula State Park★** *(Off Wis. 42. 920-868-3258. Naturalist hikes Mem. Day–Labor Day; adm. fee)*, a popular recreation area where you can rent Windsurfers, hike scenic coastal trails, play golf, or attend a show by the American Folklore Theatre *(mid-June–Aug.; adm. fee)*, which produces musicals with local history themes.

Continue to the city of **❺ Green Bay** *(Convention & Visitors Bureau 920-494-9507 or 888-867-3342)*, the state's oldest non-Indian settlement, and originally a trading post for the fur industry. When explorer Jean Nicolet claimed Green Bay for France in 1634, resident Indians gave a feast at which 120 beavers were served. By the 1680s, Green Bay was a prosperous community of missionaries, French traders, trappers, and Indians. The juncture of railroad and shipping lines has kept the city an important manufacturing center, but the most significant event after Nicolet's feast was probably the arrival of the Green Bay Packers football team in 1919.

Native dress at Oneida Nation Museum, near Green Bay

The **Green Bay Packer Hall of Fame★★** *(855 Lombardi Ave., by Lambeau Field. 920-499-4281. Adm. fee)* is not so much a museum as a shrine. In addition to displays on great Packer teams, there are videos of legendary football games including the "Ice Bowl" of 1967, and a net-surrounded area where kids of any age can punt and throw. From June through August, tour Lambeau Field, and visit the press box and playing field. Across the street is the practice field, where fans watch their heroes train from mid-July until the season starts. To get in the mood, pick up a Styrofoam "cheesehead" at the gift shop.

Not far from Packer paradise stands the **National Railroad Museum★** *(2285 S. Broadway. 920-437-7623. Train*

rides May–mid-Oct.; adm. fee), one of the country's better historical railroad yards. Situated along the Fox River, the museum grounds are home to more than 70 locomotives and engines, including the world's largest steam engine.

Also along the river, **Heritage Hill State Historical Park** *(2640 S. Webster Ave. 920-448-5150 or 800-721-5150. Mem. Day–Labor Day Tues.-Sun., Sept. weekends; adm. fee)* covers different eras of Wisconsin history, with costumed interpreters at many of the 25 historical buildings, ranging from a 1762 fur trader's cabin to a 1900s brick farmhouse. Back toward the bay, the excellent **Neville Public Museum★** *(210 Museum Pl. 920-448-4460. Closed Mon.; donation)* allows you to enter a cave mouth and time-travel 12,000 years; as you visit the ice age, you'll encounter some loud woolly mammoths. Science, history, and art exhibits from the museum's extensive collections fill the galleries.

The Great Fire of 1871 swept up the west shore of Green Bay, leaving a path of destruction 40 miles long and 10 miles wide in four hours. Towns that made a living off timber were suddenly consumed by forest fires. Visitors with an interest in the cataclysm can detour north on US 41 to **Peshtigo,** where 800 residents were killed in the tragedy. Many victims were buried at the Peshtigo Fire Cemetery, next door to the **Peshtigo Fire Museum** *(400 Oconto Ave. 715-582-3244. Mem. Day–early Oct.; donation)*, which features dusty historical exhibits and a dramatic mural depicting the fire.

111

Wooden longhouse, Oneida Nation Museum

Return south through Green Bay, and head west via County Road G, and south on County Road E to the **Oneida Nation Museum★** *(W892 Cty. Rd. EE, De Pere. 920-869-2768. May-Oct. Tues.-Sun., Nov.-April Tues.-Fri.; adm. fee)*. The Oneida were among several New York–area tribes led by missionaries to the Fox River Valley in the 1820s to escape white encroachment; upon their arrival, they found themselves competing with other Indians and whites for land. Their traditional culture is described at the museum, where visitors step inside a longhouse and handle drums, dolls, and tools used to grind corn.

Go west on County Road EE and follow Wis. 55 north to the city of **Seymour** *(Chamber of Commerce*

920-833-6053), if you want to pay homage to that most American of foods, the hamburger. Locals claim that the disk of ground beef got its name here in 1885 from a food merchant known as Hamburger Charlie. To underline Seymour's importance in burger history, the city earned a listing in the *Guinness Book of World Records* by cooking a 5,520-pounder on a huge outdoor grill in 1989. Visit the funky **Hamburger Hall of Fame**★ *(126 N. Main St. 920-833-9522. Mem. Day–Labor Day; donation)*, or come the first weekend in August to the annual Burger Fest, featuring events such as the ketchup slide and the bun toss.

Dip south to **Appleton** *(Convention & Visitors Bureau 920-734-3358 or 800-236-6673)* for a visit to the **Houdini Historical Center** *(330 E. College Ave. 920-733-8445. Mem. Day–Labor Day daily, Labor Day–Mem. Day Tues.-Sun.; adm. fee)*, part of the fortresslike **Outagamie Museum.** In addition to pictures and memorabilia of Houdini's life, the museum has artifacts such as the handcuffs put on President James Garfield's assassin...from which Houdini, later on, was able to slip free. In the summer magicians perform. The yellow-brick, Victorian **Hearthstone**★ *(625 W. Prospect Ave. 920-730-8204. Mem. Day–Labor Day Tues.-Fri. and Sun., Labor Day–Mem. Day Tues., Thurs., and Sun.; adm. fee)* was the first home electrified by a central hydroelectric plant. In addition to its fine tile- and woodwork, the mansion displays Thomas Edison light switches, electric chandeliers, and a children's hands-on electricity display.

Head farther south on US 41 to ❻ **Oshkosh** *(Convention & Visitors Bureau 920-236-5250 or 800-876-5250)*, once known as "Sawdust City" for its many woodworking shops. The economy diversified (ever heard of Oshkosh B'Gosh overalls?), and Lake Winnebago is now a popular vacation stop. Wander the gardens of the **Paine Art Center and Arboretum**★★ *(1410 Algoma Blvd. 920-235-6903.*

Antique aircraft at annual Fly-In Convention, Oshkosh

Closed Mon.; adm. fee)—from the precise geometry of the English-style sunken garden to the enormous bur oak that shades the house. Among the artworks within the 1920s Tudor Revival structure are paintings by French masters, etchings by James McNeill Whistler, and sculpture by Frederic Remington.

A sizable number of Oshkosh visitors drop out of the sky for the annual Experimental Aircraft Association Fly-In Convention, which draws more than 15,000 aircraft in early August to Wittman Regional Airport. Year-round, fliers visit the EAA's **Air Adventure Museum**★★ *(3000 Poberezny Rd. 920-426-4800. Adm. fee)*. The huge facility holds historic aircraft such as a replica of *Voyager*, the lightweight carbon-fiber plane that was first to circle the globe without landing; a working replica of the Wright brothers' *Flyer*; and warplanes of various vintages. Visitors can take flights *(daily in summer, weekends rest of year)* in open cockpit biplanes at the Pioneer Airport, a re-creation of an old-time airport.

Kettle Moraine State Forest

The road between Fond du Lac and Sheboygan was once a plank road (now Wis. 23), and in the 1850s travelers often broke up the journey at Sylvanus Wade's inn in **Greenbush.** Visitors to the **Wade House State Historic Site** and the 1860s **Stagecoach Inn** *(W7747 Plank Rd. 920-526-3271. May-Oct.; adm. fee)* can ride horse-drawn wagons *(fare)* to the **Wesley Jung Carriage Museum** to look at 19th-century hand- and horse-drawn vehicles.

Turn south on County Road T and pick up the marked Kettle Moraine Scenic Drive for a journey through **Kettle Moraine State Forest**★ *(920-626-2116. Use fee)*, where roads and trails explore the ridges and depressions left by retreating glaciers over 10,000 years ago. Set high on one of the glacial moraines, the **Henry S. Reuss Ice Age Visitor Center** *(0.5 mile S of Dundee, on Wis. 67. 920-533-8322)* has exhibits on how the glaciers sculptured Wisconsin; there are naturalist talks and guided tours from spring to autumn. The forest offers many options for bicyclists, skiers, and hikers, including a 29-mile segment of the Ice Age National Scenic Trail (see sidebar page 108).

Return to Port Washington by heading south on Wis. 67 and US 45, and east on Wis. 33.

Milwaukee to the Dells★

● **510 miles** ● **3 to 5 days** ● **Spring through autumn**
● **Taliesin is open May through Oct.** ● **Wisconsin Dells can be congested in summer.**

Taking in the industrial grit and vigor of Milwaukee, the green marshes of central Wisconsin, and the grassy dairy lands of the state's southern tier, this journey crosses a varied landscape. After exploring Milwaukee's breweries, mansions, and cultural sights, the drive zigzags through cow country, stopping at the state capital and lively university town, Madison. Then it's west to the Mississippi River, and up into Frank Lloyd Wright's stomping grounds at Spring Green. From there, the route wends to Circus World in Baraboo and the carnival-like atmosphere of Wisconsin Dells. The final stop is Horicon Marsh, a reminder that 12,000 years ago this part of the state was the turf of mile-high glaciers.

With the recent shutdown of the Pabst Brewery, ❶ **Milwaukee**'s *(Convention & Visitors Bureau 414-273-7222 or 800-231-0903)* future fame will have to be built on something other than beer. Advertising slogans aside, the city has always had a diverse economy, producing everything from the shovels that dug the Panama Canal to butter-almond toffee. The last big brewery in town is the **Miller Brewing Company**★ *(4251 W. State St. 414-931-BEER. Tours Mon.-Sat.),* where they still claim to use a strain of yeast introduced by Frederic Miller in 1855. Miller survived Prohibition selling cereal drinks and malt tonic, and now this largely automated plant produces 500,000 cases of beer a day. Beer was once kept cool underground, beneath the plant, in what is now the Caves Museum, which displays old tools and bottles.

Pabst left a bitter aftertaste in Milwaukee when it announced it was shutting its brewery *(915 W. Juneau Ave.)*, but the battlements and castlelike exterior of its closed complex are worth a drive by.

Times were better in 1892, when Capt. Frederick Pabst built his mansion amid a line of lavish houses on Grand Avenue. Designed in the Flemish Renaissance Revival

Storm clouds over Milwaukee

style, the **Pabst Mansion**★★ *(2000 W. Wisconsin Ave. 414-931-0808. Adm. fee)* boasts such extravagances as linen wallpaper soaked in linseed oil, ornately carved woodwork, delft tiles in the kitchen, and extraordinary ironwork.

The industrial success of Milwaukee has paid the bills for a thriving arts community, dating back to the 1895 **Capt. Frederick Pabst Theater**★ *(144 E. Wells St. 414-286-3665. Tour Sat. 11:30 a.m.)*, which still hosts theater and music performances. The **Charles Allis Art Museum**★ *(1801 N. Prospect Ave. 414-278-8295. Wed.-Sun.; adm. fee)* displays the paintings and objets d'art collected by industrialist Charles Allis from Asia, Europe, and America. On the bluffs above Lake Michigan stands the charming **Villa Terrace**★ *(2220 N. Terrace Ave. 414-271-3656. Wed.-Sun.; adm. fee)*, designed by architect David Adler with a walled sculpture court-yard and formal gardens. The museum is devoted to the decorative arts, with displays of paintings, furniture, and rugs from four centuries. Many of the items at Villa

Brew tank, Miller Brewing Company

Inside a geodesic dome, Mitchell Park Conservatory

Cold Hard Facts

116

Visitors to Wisconsin may find that conversations in this glacier-carved landscape are laced with the odd-sounding lingo of glaciologists. Here's a brief glossary:

Drift–rock left behind by a glacier.

Drumlin–a blunt-nose, elongated hill smoothed by a glacier.

Esker–a snakelike ridge left by a glacier.

Kames–conical hills smoothed by glaciers.

Kettle–a bowl-shaped depression caused by melting ice blocks.

Moraine–a mound of till left behind by a glacier.

Nunatak–a solitary knob that was once surrounded by glaciers.

Striae–parallel lines gouged by rocks in the base of a retreating glacier.

Terrace are from the extensive ancient and modern collections of the **Milwaukee Art Museum** ★ *(750 N. Lincoln Memorial Dr. 414-224-3200. Closed Mon.; adm. fee)*, located on the lakefront in the War Memorial Center.

Other lakeside downtown sights include the modern **Milwaukee Public Museum** *(800 W. Wells St. 414-278-2700. Adm. fee)*, which whisks visitors from a tropical rain forest to old Milwaukee, and the nearby **Betty Brinn Children's Museum**★ *(929 E. Wisconsin Ave. 414-291-0888. June-Aug. daily, Sept.-May Tues.-Sun.)*, with hands-on exhibits that let children crawl around in a "Play Port," make juice from a metal apple tree, and try their hands at running a bank.

At Marquette University stands the 15th-century **St. Joan of Arc Chapel** *(14th St. and Wisconsin Ave. 414-288-6873)*, which was dismantled in Lyon, France, and eventually reconstructed here in 1965. Wisconsin native Frank Lloyd Wright designed a quite different setting for worship on the edge of the city, the disk-shaped **Annunciation Greek Orthodox Church**★ *(9400 W. Congress St., Wauwatosa. 414-461-9400. Call for appt.)*.

Another highlight is the **Mitchell Park Conservatory** *(524 S. Layton Blvd. 414-649-9800. Adm. fee)*, with its three geodesic domes—one with tropical plants, another with desert vegetation, and a third with changing shows. A more conventional, but still beautiful, display of horticulture awaits at the **Boerner Botanical Gardens** ★ *(Whitnall Park, 5879 S. 92nd St. 414-425-1132. Parking fee)*.

Head south and west from Milwaukee via I-43, Wis. 83, Wis. 99, and County Road NN, to Eagle and the southern unit of the **Kettle Moraine State Forest** *(Wis. 59. 414-594-6200. Adm. fee)*. The forest is marked by distinctive glacial features such as kames and eskers, with backpacking shelters along the Ice Age National Scenic Trail (see sidebar page 108), and a shooting range for archery and firearms. Just beyond Eagle, old farmhouses and town buildings from around the state have been assembled into ethnic and historical clusters at **Old World Wisconsin**★ *(Wis. 67. 414-594-6300. May-Oct.; adm. fee)*. Old World is still expanding; right now, German, Danish, Finnish, and Norwegian lifestyles are represented.

Proceed southwest on Wis. 67, Wis. 11, and US 14 to
❷ **Janesville,** where Abraham Lincoln spent two nights
in 1859 at the 26-room William Tallman House, now the
Lincoln-Tallman Restorations *(440 N. Jackson St. 608-
756-4509 or 800-577-1859. June-Sept. daily, Oct.-May weekends; adm. fee).* The Italianate house and other buildings
are open for guided tours. Janesville is also home to an
enormous, 75-year-old General Motors truck plant
(1000 Industrial Ave. 608-756-7681. Tours Mon.-Thurs.). The
assembly line robots and lasers are recent innovations.

Continue north to peaceful **Aztalan State Park** *(N on
Wis. 26, W on Cty. Rd. B, S on Cty. Rd. Q. 920-648-8774. May-
Oct.).* A thousand years ago Indians grew corn and squash
and built a stockade in the rolling hills here facing the
Crawfish River. They disappeared mysteriously around
A.D. 1200; people once believed they traveled to Mexico
and became the Aztecs—hence the park's name. Some
artifacts are kept at the **Aztalan Historical Museum** *(920-
648-8845. Mid-May–Sept.; adm. fee),* which is adjacent to the
park and mainly dedicated to the history of white settlers
who arrived later.

117

Drive west on I-94, and take US 151 south to reach a
narrow isthmus between
Lakes Monona and Men-
dota, site of the state capital, ❸ **Madison**★★
*(Convention & Visitors
Bureau 608-255-2537 or
800-373-6376).* A city
often cited as one of the
best places to live in the
country, it offers recre-
ation on the lakes and in
the city center at **Vilas
Park,** next to the **Henry
Vilas Zoo** *(702 S. Randall
Ave. 608-266-4732).* It also
boasts the highly rated

Oxen pulling a plow, Old World Wisconsin, near Eagle

University of Wisconsin and hip student hangouts along
State Street. At the top of that street is the white granite
Wisconsin State Capitol★★ *(608-266-0382),* with elabo-
rate friezes on its pediments, and statuary and panels of
artwork throughout.

On Capitol Square stands the **State Historical
Museum**★ *(30 N. Carroll St. 608-264-6555. Closed Mon.),* with
exhibits on four floors that describe Wisconsin's Indian
tribes, and the state's political history, which spawned

populist movements like the Progressive Party in the 1930s.

The **University of Wisconsin** *(608-263-2400)* has a reputation for top-notch academics and lively political activism. It also has a beautiful setting with its own stretch of Lake Mendota shore. For fine art dating back as far as 2300 B.C. visit the university's **Elvehjem Museum of Art** *(800 University Ave. 608-263-2246. Closed Mon.)*. Mastodon and dinosaur skeletons are displayed in the **Geology Museum** *(1215 W. Dayton St. 608-262-2399. Mon.-Sat.)*. Inspired by the late Frank Lloyd Wright in 1938, a new convention center with a dramatic arcade facing Lake Monona finally opened in 1997. Wright also designed the striking **First Unitarian Society Meeting House** *(900 University Bay Dr. 608-233-9774. May-Sept. Mon.-Sat.; donation)*.

Leave town on US 18 west toward **Blue Mounds,** named for the blue hue of the two highest hills in south-

State Capitol, Madison

ern Wisconsin. Nestled in a green valley called Nissedahle, or "valley of the elves," you'll find **Little Norway** *(3576 Cty. Rd. JG, off US 18. 608-437-8211. May-Oct.; adm. fee)*. Among the 1856 homestead farm buildings here, all furnished with Norse antiques, are a sod-roof cabin and a reconstructed 12th-century Stavkirke with carved dragons at its gable peaks. Not far away, **Cave of the Mounds** *(2975 Cave of the Mounds Rd. 608-437-3038. Mid-March–mid-Nov. daily, mid-Nov.–mid-March weekends; adm. fee)* is a limestone cavern located beneath the East Mound, filled with a variety of galleries and formations.

Cornish miners were among the immigrants drawn to southern Wisconsin in the 19th century when lead ore was discovered at **Mineral Point**★ *(Chamber of Commerce 608-987-3201 or 888-POINT-WI)*, to the southwest and reached by following US 151. Their limestone and log cottages were restored in the 1930s by two men who opened a cozy Cornish restaurant. Today **Pendarvis Historic Site**★ *(114 Shake Rag St. 608-987-2122. May-Oct.;*

adm. fee) is a rambling collection of cottages and gardens connected by rock paths. Interpreters in costume tell the story of the Cornish immigrants. The creative spirit that revived Pendarvis has pervaded all of Mineral Point, where the steep streets are filled with the galleries of weavers, potters, and other artisans.

Continue on US 151 to **Platteville,** where the **Mining Museum** *(405 E. Main St. 608-348-3301. May-Oct.; adm. fee)* offers a firsthand look at how zinc and lead were removed in these parts. You can climb down into the Bevans Lead Mine, or take an aboveground ride in ore cars pulled by a mine locomotive.

In **Dickeyville,** stop at the **Dickeyville Grotto** *(305 W. Main St. 608-568-3119. Tours daily June-Aug., weekends May and Sept.-Oct.; donation),* an inspired piece of junk artistry. Father Mathias Wernerus built the shrine in the 1920s using glass, gemstones, and petrified wood. Explored at night, the well-lit grotto transcends its primitive technique.

119

Little Norway, Nissedahle Valley

Northwest on US 61, travelers hook up with the **Great River Road,** a winding route along the Mississippi River famous for scenery that includes soaring limestone bluffs, barge traffic on the river, and marshy bayous. Near Cassville, the view from the bluffs at ❹ **Nelson Dewey State Park** *(12190 Cty. Rd. VV. 608-725-5374. Adm. fee)* takes in a wide stretch of the lazy Mississippi. Adjacent to the park is an 1890s settlement called **Stonefield Historic Site** *(608-725-5210. Mem. Day–mid-Oct.; adm. fee).* In the summer the village bustles with activity—blacksmiths hammering, merchants selling wares, and visitors milling around the 30 historical buildings.

Farther north on the Great River Road, where the Wisconsin and Mississippi Rivers join, **Wyalusing State Park** *(13342 Cty. Rd. C. 608-996-2261. Adm. fee)* offers a view of the confluence from Point Lookout, 500 feet above the river. Ancient Indians constructed mounds in the shape of turtles, bears, and birds, some of which are visible along the informative **Sentinel Ridge Nature Trail,** a 0.5-mile loop. The nearly 25 miles of trails will have hikers puffing.

Just north of the rivers' confluence sprawls **Prairie du Chien** *(Chamber of Commerce 608-326-8555 or 800-PDC-1673),* a base for John Jacob Astor's American Fur Company early in the 19th century. Hercules Dousman, an Astor agent, owned a riverside country estate called

The Wright Height

The brilliant architect Frank Lloyd Wright (1867-1959) often couldn't pay his bills. Out of necessity, he turned his Wisconsin home, Taliesin, into a school, and apprentices came from afar to learn Wright's technique of designing structures to fit a landscape. Often they ended up pounding nails next to Wright, as he expanded his rambling farm. Wright's acolytes were devoted to him—some of them continue to live and work at Taliesin today. Ducking through the low-slung entryways one wonders, though, if any of them were tall. The vertically challenged Wright, himself five feet six inches, seemed to take pleasure in making tall people "stoop to contour." The architectural genius described people over six feet tall as "an excessive use of materials."

Villa Louis★★ *(521 N. Villa Louis Rd. 608-326-2721. May-Oct.; adm. fee)*, where his son built a horse racetrack of imported crushed cork. The luxurious Italian villa-style house is furnished for the turn of the century. An Astor fur warehouse on the grounds is now the Fur Trade Museum.

Drive east along the Wisconsin River on Wis. 60 to Spring Green, where Frank Lloyd Wright returned to his roots in 1911 to build a house (see sidebar this page). From the **Frank Lloyd Wright Visitor Center** *(Wis. 23 and Cty. Rd. C. 608-588-7900. May-Oct., call for off-season hours; fee for tours. Reservations recommended)*, across the river from Spring Green, walking and house tours visit Wright's home ❺ **Taliesin**★★ (Welsh for "shining brow") and the Hillside Home School. The unorthodox Wright was never popular in Spring Green, but he loved the valley. The subtle ways in which the topography and his architecture complement each other reveal themselves as you walk around.

Just down the road from Taliesin awaits the inimitable **House on the Rock**★★ *(5754 Wis. 23. 608-935-3639. Mid-March–early Oct., early Nov.–early Jan.; adm. fee)*, the flip side of Wright's ascetic genius. Built by the late Alex Jordan in the 1940s, the house violates in every way Wright's cardinal rule of fitting form to the landscape. A room thrusts out from the structure's rocky roost like a dagger over the forest below, and kitschy junk spills over everywhere. A series of huge, themed rooms hold increasingly extravagant and daffy exhibits that include sea monsters, brewing vats, and bare-breasted angels above the world's largest carousel. The madder it gets, the more strangely gladdening it feels.

Return north on Wis. 23, heading east on Wis. 60, north on US 12, and west on County Road C to **Natural Bridge State Park**★ *(Cty. Rd. C. 608-356-8301. Mid-April–Oct.; adm. fee)*, where, if you've just visited House on the Rock, you can compare nature's work to man's. The sandstone bridge measures 35 feet across and 25 feet high.

Now proceed north on US 12 to ❻ **Baraboo,** where the Ringling Brothers Circus wintered from 1884 to 1918. The grounds of the old circus home are now the **Circus World Museum**★★ *(426 Water St. 608-356-0800. Visitor Center open daily, outdoor entertainment May–early Sept.; adm. fee)*. In the summer, visitors wander through exhibits and inspect over 150 circus wagons on the grounds before ducking into the Big Top tent for a variety of circus acts.

A short distance north of Baraboo you'll find the **International Crane Foundation**★ *(E-11376 Shady Lane Rd.*

608-356-9462. *May-Oct.; adm. fee)*, dedicated to protecting and studying cranes. Five-foot-tall whooping cranes can be viewed in a natural prairie marsh environment, and visitors touring the facility can see crane chicks being fed (they hatch from May to October).

Continue north on US 12 to **Wisconsin Dells** *(Visitors Bureau 608-254-4636 or 800-22-DELLS)*, and brace yourself. One resident describes it as "the most visually polluted vacation area in the U.S." She may be right about the town, which is jammed with carnival-like water-theme parks and attractions, but the Dells themselves—7 miles of sandstone cliffs along the Wisconsin River—retain their natural beauty. A favorite way to view the Dells is aboard a "duck" *(Original Wisconsin Ducks, 1890 Wisconsin Dells Pkwy. 608-254-8751. April-Oct.; fare)*, the amphibious World War II crafts that navigate trails and river, or on boat tours of the Upper and Lower Dells *(Dells Boat Tours, 11 Broadway. 608-254-8555. April-late Oct.; fare)*.

House on the Rock, near Spring Green

121

Billboards hawk various attractions along Wisconsin Dells Parkway—from the waterskiing performances in the **Tommy Bartlett Thrill Show** *(560 Wisconsin Dells Pkwy. 608-254-2525. Mem. Day–Labor Day; adm. fee)* to **Big Chief's Karts and Coasters World** *(1881 Wisconsin Dells Pkwy. 608-254-2490. Daily mid-May–mid-Sept., weekends April–mid-May and mid-Sept.–Oct.; adm. fee)*.

If you get away from the glitter of "the Strip," there is great natural beauty in the Baraboo Range. You can hike, or take a fall-color trip on the **Mid-Continent Railway** *(Off Wis. 136 on Cty. Rd. PF, North Freedom. 608-522-4261. Mem. Day–Labor Day daily, early Sept.–mid-Oct. weekends; fare)*. And if you plan far ahead, you could spend a night in the Frank Lloyd Wright-designed **Seth Peterson Cottage** *(US 12, Mirror Lake State Park. 608-254-6551)* on a promontory above Mirror Lake.

Carnival characters, Circus World Museum

Drive east on Wis. 16 and Wis. 33 to ❼ **Horicon Marsh**★ *(920-387-7860)*, the nation's largest freshwater cattail marsh. Enthusiasts tour the marsh in canoes and pontoon boats *(call marsh for outfitter information)*. This is an important stop for migrating Canada geese and more than 250 other bird species.

To return to Milwaukee, take Wis. 33 and US 41.

North Woods and the Apostles

● 500 miles ● 3 to 5 days ● Spring through autumn

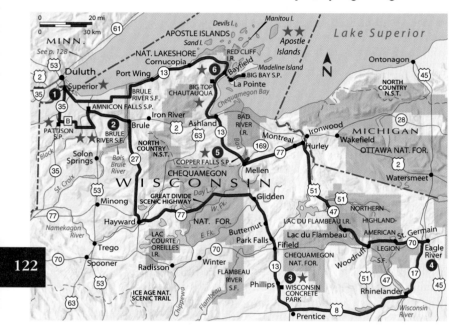

Wisconsin owns a small but magical stretch of Lake Superior real estate, indented by a deep harbor at Superior and crowned by the Apostle Islands. South of the Lake Superior shore lie the lake-dotted North Woods, where coffee shop talk often hinges on duck decoys, or that tall pike Shorty caught over the weekend. The towering virgin forests that once covered most of Wisconsin were chopped down during the logging frenzy of the late 19th century, but, happily, conservation has nurtured a woodlands comeback.

Beginning at the town of Superior, the tour loops inland south and east through woods and across tumbling streams, with stops for some whimsical roadside attractions. Outdoor adventurers can float and fish the rivers and lakes, or hike trails leading to waterfalls and campgrounds, following in the wake of Indians who once paddled the marshes—and lumberjacks who brought down the big trees. Stories of these forerunners are told by the small museums along the way. Returning to the lakeshore, hop a ferry or sailboat to the Apostles for a dose of natural beauty.

Over a century ago, when freighters started ferrying grain, timber, and minerals across the lakes, the deep water port between Duluth, Minnesota (see North Shore Loop drive, p. 128), and the small Wisconsin city of **❶ Superior**★ *(Chamber of Commerce 715-392-2773 or 800-942-5313)* began to thrive. Boosters call it an "inland ocean port," since the St. Lawrence Seaway connects it to the Atlantic Ocean. Take US 2 and US 53 to Barkers Island, where you can take a narrated cruise from the dock to see the shipyards, Aerial Lift Bridge, and ships loading and unloading at the **Duluth-Superior Harbor**★ *(Vista Fleet, Barkers Island Dock. 715-394-6846. Mid-May–mid-Oct.; fare)*. Also on Barkers Island is the 1896 **SS Meteor and Maritime Museum** *(715-392-5742. Mid-May–mid-Oct.; adm. fee)*, housed in a unique "whaleback" freighter with a rounded, low-rider design that let stormy weather wash right over it. Now landlocked, the museum has exhibits on shipbuilding and Great Lakes maritime lore.

Across from Barkers Island, on the mainland, awaits **Fairlawn Mansion** *(906 E. 2nd St. 715-394-5712. Closed for renovation until early 1998; adm. fee)*, a 42-room, tower-topped Victorian built by timber-and-mining magnate Martin Pattison. The house has period furnishings on the first floor, a museum on the second and third floors, and a small, comforting wildflower arbor outside.

123

It's a short drive south on Wis. 35 to **Pattison State Park**★ *(6294 S. Wis. 35. 715-399-3111. Adm. fee)*, where the Black

SS Meteor and Maritime Museum, Barkers Island

River roars over 165-foot Big Manitou Falls. This is just your first taste of the wild North Woods, which stretch across the state's northern half toward Lake Michigan and are protected by a patchwork of parks, Indian reservations, and national, state, and county forests. Pattison State Park has lakeside beaches, campgrounds, and hiking trails. Another piece of the North Woods mosaic sprawls off US 2 in **Amnicon Falls State Park** *(Cty. Rd. U. 715-398-3000. May–early Oct.; adm. fee)*, which also has spectacular waterfalls.

An ancient Indian portage route ran between the Mississippi River system at Upper St. Croix Lake and Lake Superior, by way of the Bois Brule River, now surrounded by **❷ Brule River State Forest**★★ *(715-372-4866)*. High sandstone bluffs rise above the gabbro-and-sandstone-lined river. Trout fishing *(license required)* here has lured Presidents from Ulysses S. Grant to Dwight D. Eisenhower. The river begins in the broad, spring-fed valley of the upper Bois Brule, then speeds up in the lower river, with moderate rapids for white-water enthusiasts *(call park for information).*

Proceed to **Hayward** on Wis. 27, home of the **National Fresh Water Fishing Hall of Fame** ★ *(1 Hall of Fame Dr. 715-634-4440. Mid-April–Oct.; adm. fee),* where you can stand in the jaws of the world's largest (steel-and-fiberglass) muskie. It probably takes a confirmed fishing addict to appreciate the Wing of Outboard Motors, but other exhibits pique interest in Wisconsin's many fish species, as well as old-time tackle and gear.

The route moves east along Wis. 77 and onto the Great Divide Scenic Byway, which offers 30 miles of dense forest scenery through **Chequamegon National Forest** *(Great Divide District Office 715-634-4821).* This is the divide from which waters go north to the Gulf of St. Lawrence, or south to the Gulf of Mexico. Maples and aspens provide fall color. Along the route are canoe drop-ins on the West Fork Chippewa River, biking and hiking trails, and campground and swimming areas at Day Lake. Keep eyes peeled for bald eagles near the road.

120-foot muskie, National Fresh Water Fishing Hall of Fame

The loggers who cut down the timber in these parts were not without aesthetic sense—the late Fred Smith, for instance, retired his chain saw in 1949 and took up concrete sculpture. To see his eccentric art, turn south on Wis. 13 just before Glidden. Smith built 250 life-size owls, cowboys, and other figures embellished with glass and mirrors—all on display in forest glades at the ❸ **Wisconsin Concrete Park** ★ *(Wis. 13, Phillips. 715-339-6371. Adm. fee).*

Farther south on Wis. 13 and east on US 8 lies **Rhinelander** *(Chamber of Commerce 715-362-7464),* where life in a logging camp for Smith and his cohorts was no walk in the park. The **Rhinelander Logging Museum** ★ *(Pioneer Park, Oneida Ave. 715-369-5004. Mid-May–mid-Sept.; donation)* re-creates the living quarters, tools, and cook's shack that were a timber cutter's world. There is also a

marvelous mechanical scale-model sawmill and shingle mill, with 8-inch figures hard at work. The mountainous country around Rhinelander is buttoned with lakes and stitched with trails for hikers and snowmobilers.

Head north on Wis. 17 to **❹ Eagle River** *(Information Bureau 715-479-8575 or 800-359-6315)*, where a string of resort-lined lakes reel in fishermen. Cranberries grow in the bogs around the lakes, and in early October there is a cranberry celebration. In winter, chilly Eagle River becomes a snowmobile hot spot, both for its network of forest trails and its world championship *(late Jan.)* and endurance races held on its oval track *(Wis. 45. 715-479-4424. Adm. fee)*. Snowmobilers will want to stop at the **International Snowmobile Racing Hall of Fame and Museum** *(Wis. 70, 1 mile E of St. Germain. 715-359-3463. Mon.-Fri.)* for a look at videos and some ancient (1967) snowmobiles.

Drive west on Wis. 70, and briefly south on US 51. At Woodruff, pick up Wis. 47 through the Lac du Flambeau Indian Reservation, named by French trappers for the torches used by Ojibwe for night fishing. A few blocks from the spanking new **Lake of the Torches Resort/Casino** *(510 Old Abe Rd. 715-588-7070 or 800-25-TORCH)*, in the town of **Lac du Flambeau,** stands the **George W. Brown, Jr. Ojibwe Museum & Cultural Center★** *(603 Peace Pipe Rd. 715-588-3333. May-Oct. Mon.-Sat., Nov.-April Tues.-Thurs.; adm. fee)*, with dioramas showing the traditional Ojibwe way of life. There are displays of beadwork, and a dugout canoe (believed to be over 250 years old) that was lifted from the bottom of a lake.

Continue to **❺ Copper Falls State Park★** *(Wis. 169. 715-274-5123. Adm. fee)*, a geological jumble of granite, clay, basalt, and sandstone gouged into steep-walled canyons by the Bad River. Eight miles of hiking trails run through the 2,800-acre park, including a section of the **North Country National Scenic Trail,** en route from New York to North Dakota.

Backtrack to Wis. 13 and follow it north to the Lake Superior coast at **Ashland** *(Chamber of Commerce 715-682-2500)*, deep in the curve of Chequamegon Bay. Sawmills and stone quarries were the livelihood here a century ago, and that history is told at the **Northern Wisconsin History Center** *(Relocating in early 1998. 715-682-6600. By appt.; adm. fee)*. One of the largest oredocks in the world, the Soo Line Oredock *(Water St.)* pokes into the bay, no longer in use but worth a look for maritime nostalgia.

North of Ashland on Wis. 13, the Bayfield Peninsula juts into Lake Superior, topped by a scattering of islands

---

Muskie Fever

The respect with which fishermen talk about the muskellunge—"muskie" to friends (and foes)—is matched only by the reverence with which Wisconsinites utter the word "Packers." To many, the true measure of an angler is a tussle with this fierce tackle-mangler. The world record catch weighed 69 pounds 11 ounces. If you're lusting for muskie, troll a bucktail lure in the spring, an artificial "jerk bait" in the summer, or a live suckerfish in the fall. Tell the youngsters to keep their hands in the boat—every year there are stories about a muskie snapping at a dangling finger. Though muskies are not easily snared, many anglers find the pleasure of floating along the lakes in the midst of fall color to be more than just reward.

125

North Woods and the Apostles

Devils Island

The Apostle Islands huddle together on Wisconsin's north shore, a protective haven with bays and sandy beaches where sailors once fled the ferocity of Lake Superior storms. Over the centuries Ojibwe, French trappers, and Midwesterners on summer vacation have all sought refuge here. But one of the Apostles, Devils Island, is no saintly sanctuary. Wisconsin's northernmost point, it has no barrier to shield its north end from the ferocious winds and waves. The result is a battered coast of catacombed cliffs, shaped by relentless erosion into spires and arches and caves. Tour boats from Bayfield coast by the caves, and small boats can actually enter some of them, where the amplified echoes of water slapping the recesses of the chambers can be heard. Keep an eye on the weather when you make this trip, and return safely to the cloistered comfort of the inner islands.

that look as if they were broken off when the lake bit down on the shore. The result is the **Apostle Islands National Lakeshore** ★ ★, one of the state's treasures. A visit to the Apostles begins in the fishing port of ❻ **Bayfield** ★ *(Chamber of Commerce 715-779-3335 or 800-447-4094)*. Note that just south of town you'll find the **Big Top Chautauqua** ★ *(Ski Hill Rd. 715-373-5552 or 888-BIG-TENT. June–Labor Day, call for schedule; adm. fee)*, a summer series of music, drama, and talk modeled on the traveling tent shows of a century ago.

A cooper was once as important as a blacksmith or a barber. The art of making barrels survives today at **Bayfield's Cooperage Museum** *(1 Washington Ave. 715-779-5076. Mid-May–mid-Oct.)*, where a craftsman shapes staves to fit barrel hoops. The museum is squeezed next to **Trek & Trail** *(715-779-3585)*, a canoe-and-kayak outfitter that offers kayak lessons and guided trips to the Apostles that explore sea caves, shipwrecks, and lighthouses.

Before you lift a paddle or hoist a sail, climb the hill to the **Apostle Islands National Lakeshore Visitor Center** *(Washington Ave. and 4th St. 715-779-3397. May-Oct. daily, Nov.-April Mon.-Fri.)*, which provides information on the islands, as well as camping permits. All but one of the Apostle Islands comprise a national lakeshore administered by the National Park Service.

The one island that is not part of the national lakeshore is the biggest, and the only one with restaurants, roads, and motels: **Madeline Island** *(Chamber of Commerce 715-747-2801 or 800-ISLE-FUN)*. From spring thaw until the lake freezes, usually in late December, a car ferry *(Madeline Island Ferry Line 715-747-2051. Fare)* makes the 20-minute journey from Bayfield to La Pointe and back, with departures every half hour in summer. **La Pointe** was a center for the Indian, French, and English fur trade from the 17th century to about 1840. That history is told at the **Madeline Island Historical Museum** ★ *(La Pointe. 715-747-2415. Mem. Day–early Oct.; adm. fee)*, which has ancient Ojibwe artifacts such as a cranberry picker and a war club. If you want to get around the island, rent a bike or moped by the docks *(call Madeline Island Chamber of Commerce for information)* or take the **Madeline Island Bus Tour** *(Next to ferry dock. 715-747-2051. Mid-June–Aug.; fare)*.

A barrier beach encloses a sandy lagoon at **Big Bay State Park** *(Cty. Rd. H to Hagen Rd. 715-747-6425. Adm. fee)*, which conjoins Big Bay Town Park. Despite warnings against the chill of Superior's waters, you'll find a few brave

souls immersed here, and in some of the small coves off
the trails that wind around Big Bay Point. Others lie on
the sand, camp, explore the seashore and bogs, or fish.

There are numerous options for adventure on the
Apostle Islands—you can float by the sea caves carved
into the north shore of **Devils Island** (see sidebar
page 126), or tour the 1881 brownstone **Sand Island**

Apostle Islands National Lakeshore

Lighthouse *(Mid-June–early Sept.)* with a volunteer guide,
or visit a restored fishing camp *(mid-June–early Sept.)* on
Manitou Island. There are docks and a limited number of
designated campsites on many of the islands. The **Apostle Islands Cruise Service** *(City Dock, Bayfield. 715-779-
3925 or 800-323-7619. Mid-May–mid-Oct.; fare)* offers day
cruises with narration on geology and maritime lore, as
well as sailing trips on a three-masted schooner. A number of other outfitters provide sail, powerboat, and fishing
charters *(call Bayfield Chamber of Commerce).*

Return to Superior by following Wis. 13.

● **740 miles** ● **5 to 6 days** ● **May to Oct.** ● **Photo identification with proof of citizenship but no passport required at Canadian border.** ● **Permits needed for canoe trips in Boundary Waters Canoe Area Wilderness and Quetico Provincial Park.**

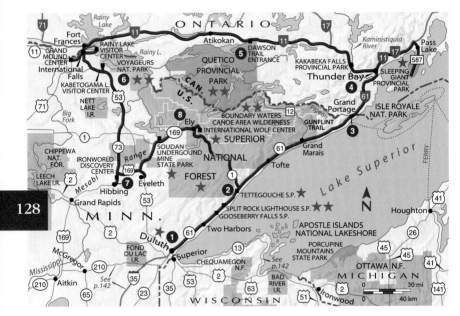

Northeast Minnesota and the Canadian realm just across the border embrace a wilderness fastness of rugged Lake Superior shoreline and lake-dotted forest, where a latter-day voyageur can go for days hearing only the dip of the paddle, the cry of the loon, and the howl of the wolf. As you take this long voyage up the Lake Superior coast and around an enormous maze of lakes and evergreen forest, you'll see fascinating evidence of man's struggle against an intimidating environment to harvest a wealth of natural resources, from furs to timber to minerals. You'll climb lighthouse towers on craggy cliffs, visit frontier outposts where voyageurs and Native Americans traded beaver pelts, and travel down an iron ore mine shaft in the Mesabi Range for a firsthand look at the diggings.

The iron ore from the Mesabi was shipped to **❶ Duluth** ★ *(Visitors Bureau 218-722-4011 or 800-438-5884)*, the robust commercial center where this journey begins. To get a sailor's perspective, ride on a sight-seeing cruise with **Vista Fleet** *(5th Ave. W. and Harbor Dr., at Convention Center Dock. 218-722-6218 or 800-438-5884. May-Oct.;*

fare) around the harbor, passing beneath the Aerial Lift Bridge as it rises and falls at the entry to Duluth Harbor. Or you can hoof it, which is a pleasure along Duluth's cheerful waterfront. Begin at the **Depot** *(506 W. Michigan St. 218-727-8025. Single adm. fee for all museums)*, an 1892 railroad station that now houses a children's museum, an art institute, the St. Louis County Historical Society displays, and the marvelous **Lake Superior Museum of Transportation**★ *(218-733-7590).* The latter takes advantage of the old rails beneath the depot to bring in such rolling stock as a huge Northern Pacific Russell Snowplow. The trains are surrounded by softly lit, re-created storefronts that give visitors a glimpse of 1910 Duluth. This lower level is also the departure point for the **North Shore Scenic Railroad** *(218-722-1273 or 800-423-1273. May–mid-Oct.; fare),* running scenic trips up the Lake Superior shore to Two Harbors and points in between.

Duluth waterfront on Lake Superior

From the depot, walk or take a trolley along Harbor Drive, stopping to tour an enormous retired ore boat, the ***William A. Irvin*** *(Harbor Dr. 218-722-7876. May-Oct.; adm. fee),* which will give you a sense of the bulk of these ships—despite its size, the 1938 *Irvin* is dwarfed by today's freighters. Cross the drawbridge at the foot of the *Irvin* and walk two blocks to **Canal Park**★★ *(Bounded by Canal Park Dr. and Lake Ave.),* where restored brick warehouses full of shops stand below the Aerial Lift Bridge. If no ships are passing under the bridge *(check arrival times on the Boatwatchers Hotline 218-722-6489),* duck into the U.S. Army Corps of Engineers' **Lake Superior Maritime Visitor Center** *(218-727-2497. May-Nov. daily, Dec.-April Fri.-Sun.)* and learn about Great Lakes shipping back to the days of sailing schooners laden with grain and iron ore. Walkers can then take off on the **Lakewalk**★, which runs 3 miles north along the water.

As you depart Duluth to the north, stop at **Glensheen**★ *(3300 London Rd. 218-724-8863 or 888-348-4377. Mid-April–late Oct. daily, late Oct.–mid-April weekends; adm. fee)* to see what became of some of the wealth generated by the bustling port a century ago. The 39-room Jacobean-style estate, completed in 1908 by attorney Chester Congdon, features carved woodwork and a formal English garden.

Now begins the journey up the beautiful **North Shore Drive**★ (Minn. 61), which opened the remote and theretofore forbidding North Shore to auto traffic in the 1920s. With its steep cliffs, dense forests, waterfalls, panoramic lakeviews, and numerous state parks, this is one of Minnesota's best drives. The first stop is **Gooseberry Falls State Park** *(1300 Minn. 61. 218-834-3855. Adm. fee)*, with five waterfalls, the tallest of which is a short walk from the Visitor Center. If the river is low, walk out on the rocks of the two-tiered Lower Falls—that's 700 million-year-old lava under your feet.

Farther up the road stands **Split Rock Lighthouse**★★ *(2010 Minn. 61. 218-226-6372. Park open mid-May–mid-Oct., history center open mid-May–mid-Oct., Sat.-Sun. rest of year; adm. fee)*, a picture-postcard octagonal tower on a rock jutting 130 feet above the lake. In the early 1900s, captains of iron ore freighters dreaded this stretch of shore. After several vessels ran aground in a 1905 storm, Congress funded this lighthouse. The big Fresnel lens was retired from service in 1969, but the site, which has lured visitors since the 1920s, is now a state park. Tour the tower, learn Great Lakes and lighthouse lore at the fine History Center, and hike trails that lead into the woods and down to the shore.

Continuing north, you'll watch the coastline become more mountainous around ❷ **Tettegouche State Park**★ *(474 Minn. 61. 218-226-6365. Adm. fee)*, which has lakes, waterfalls, fall color,

Gooseberry Falls State Park

and palisades overlooking Superior. Hike to the top of Shovel Point or Palisade Head and you may see someone jump off the cliff...rock climbers often rappel down these sheer faces.

Farther along Minn. 61, stop in the Tofte Ranger

130

District Office of the **Superior National Forest**★ *(Minn. 61, Tofte. 218-663-7280)* to pick up maps and brochures for camping and hiking. Extending in a wedge shape from the Canadian border near Voyageurs National Park to the North Shore, the national forest—which includes a million acres of the Boundary Waters Canoe Area Wilderness (see page 136)—offers numerous lakeshore starting points for hikes. For those who prefer wheels to hiking boots, the **Sawbill Trail** and other roads lead deep into the forest, where there are developed campgrounds and primitive sites, and rustic resorts on adjacent lands.

Proceed to the harbor area in **Grand Marais** *(Chamber of Commerce 218-387-2524),* a pleasant stroll on a sunny day, with shops, a park, and the small **Cook County Historical Museum** *(4 S. Broadway Ave. 218-387-2883. May-Oct. daily, Sat. only rest of year; donation),* in what was formerly a lighthouse keeper's home. Its exhibits cover logging, mining, trapping, and fishing. But Grand Marais' biggest claim to fame is the **Gunflint Trail** *(Gunflint Trail Assoc., off Minn. 61. 218-387-2870 or 800-338-6932),* which is really a road (County Road 12) that runs 63 miles west into the Boundary Waters Canoe Area Wilderness. It provides access for fishing, hiking, canoeing, mountain biking, and, in winter, snowmobiling and cross-country skiing.

Split Rock Lighthouse

Near the Canadian border, the mountains made passage difficult for the 18th-century French and Indian fur traders trying to haul their beaver bounty south from Canada to the Great Lakes. To get around rapids and waterfalls near the mouth of the Pigeon River, they hiked 8.5 miles on a route called the Grand Portage, bringing their furs to the North West Company's outpost by the lake, now reconstructed at the **Grand Portage National Monument**★ *(Off Minn. 61. 218-387-2788. Mid-May–mid-Oct.; adm. fee),* in the village of ❸ **Grand Portage.** A birchbark canoe of the era is on display within the stockade, where the great hall, kitchen, and warehouse have been reconstructed and are staffed by costumed interpreters.

If you're seeking even more solitude than this quiet corner offers, hop a ferry in town to **Isle Royale,** a wild, lonely island in the middle of Lake Superior (see sidebar page 133).

On both sides of the U.S./Canada border, this is a land of dense boreal forests and steep topography carved by winding streams—the change at gas stations from gallons to liters is the most notable indication that you're entering another country. To cross into Canada you need photo identification with proof of citizenship.

❹ **Thunder Bay** *(Visitors Bureau 807-625-2149 or 800-667-8386)* is a bustling lake port marked by the looming Sleeping Giant bluff on a peninsula across the bay. You can climb the giant and take scenic drives and trails in **Sleeping Giant Provincial Park**★ *(Hwy. 587, Pass Lake. 807-977-2526).* An urban park complex in the city center features the **Soroptimist International Friendship Garden** *(Victorian Ave. and Legion Track Dr.),* with flower beds and monuments honoring nationalities including Chinese, Croatian, Dutch, and British. Walk north along a paved path by a golf course to the **Centennial Botanical Conservatory** *(1601 Dease St. 807-622-7036),* with its large greenhouse and flower beds.

Fishermen at Boundary Waters Canoe Area Wilderness

Back at the town's south end stands **Old Fort William**★★ *(King Rd., off Broadway Ave. 807-473-2344. Mid-May–mid-Oct.; adm. fee).* Tucked in a deep turn on the Kaministiquia River, this reconstructed fur-trading post bustles with the excitement of the voyageur era more than 200 years ago, when the North West Company of Montreal made it the key link between backwoods trappers and the markets back East. From the Visitor Center, travel by bus or trail to the fort itself, passing by an Ojibwe encampment. Surrounding the main square within the palisade stand more than 36 re-created buildings. Outside awaits a working farm, heritage gardens, and a busy wharf where in July and August costumed interpreters portray trading parties.

Runoff from retreating glaciers created many of the deep gorges in these mountains and left behind waterfalls including the 128-footer in **Kakabeka Falls Provincial Park** (*Trans-Canada 11/17. 807-473-9231. Adm. fee*). Though the falls have been dammed, they still take a spectacular tumble. The park also offers hiking trails and campgrounds.

Continue west on Trans-Canada 11 to the Dawson Trail entrance to ❺ **Quetico Provincial Park★ ★** (*Off Trans-Canada 11. 807-597-2735. Adm. fee*), the Canadian twin to Minnesota's Boundary Waters Canoe Area Wilderness. There is a car-accessible campground and hiking trails at Dawson Trail, but this park is mainly for people with paddles. You have a wealth of watery choices: lakes, rivers, and, if you dare, some rough white water. The water flows over the Canadian Shield, rock as old as four billion years, some of it tilted up by volcanic pressure into

Old Fort William, Thunder Bay, Ontario

steep granite faces. On these faces, ancient peoples painted their stories in red ocher pictographs, depicting moose, caribou, and humans; park staff can direct you to these paintings, though all are accessible only by boat.

The information pavillion at Dawson Trail is a good place to learn about Quetico. Compared to Boundary Waters, there are fewer permits issued and less traffic here, but you still need to arrange a permit months before your trip. The least-used area is at the center of the 1.1 million-acre park (it takes two to three days to get there).

Continue west on the Trans-Canada Highway, past lakes and marshes and streams that open up the forests. Nearing Fort Frances, the highway rides the **Noden Causeway** over the many fingers of aptly named Rainy Lake, and you might see intrepid canoeists out on the open water.

The region's abundant timber supplies the **Abitibi-Consolidated** (*427 Mowat Ave. 807-274-8878. June-Aug. Mon.-Fri. Reservations required*), a pulp and paper mill in **Fort Frances.** The rich smell of fresh-cut pine hangs in the air as the tour follows the process of turning a tree into paper. At **Pithers Point Park** (*Off Trans-Canada 11, Rainy Lake. 807-274-5502. Mid-June–Labor Day*) stands a

Isle Royale

Getting to **Isle Royale National Park** (*906-482-0984. Mid-April–Oct.; adm. fee*) is no easy matter, and that's part of what keeps it wild and unique. Ferries (*fare; contact park for schedule*) from Grand Portage, Minnesota, or Houghton and Copper Harbor on Michigan's Upper Peninsula take hours to reach Lake Superior's largest island. Once there, you're likely to meet more pesty black flies than people—fewer than 18,000 visitors arrive annually. What a treat, though, for a seeker of solitude. Over 165 miles of trails explore boreal forests, swamps, orchids, lighthouses, and fish-loaded lakes. You can camp, or stay in cabins or rooms at Rock Harbor Lodge; sight-seeing tours and boat rentals are available at the harbor.

133

re-created trading fort and a restored logging tugboat.

Follow Trans-Canada 11 across the International Bridge, back into the United States to **International Falls** *(Chamber of Commerce 218-283-9400 or 800-325-5766),* the town that frequently reports the country's lowest temperature. Weather aficionados may want to pose with the

Voyageurs National Park

22-foot thermometer in **Smokey Bear Park** *(3rd St. and 4th Ave.).* Then drive west from International Falls on Minn. 11 to the **Grand Mound Center** *(6749 Minn. 11. 218-285-3332. May–Labor Day daily, Labor Day–Oct. weekends; adm. fee),* where five earthen mounds remain from a burial ground used by Native Americans as long ago as 3000 B.C.

The Ojibwe were the latest of those peoples, and they taught European fur hunters how to navigate the maze of water and islands that now comprise ❻ **Voyageurs National Park**★ ★ *(Headquarters, 3131 US 53. 218-283-9821).* Glaciers advanced and retreated over this country, flattening any mountains but leaving behind gouges and scrapes that became lakes and rivers. Though there are hiking trails, it's easier to get around by water than by land; powerboats are prevalent, but some use sailboats or canoes. Spot the bald eagles and ospreys in the tallest trees, and fish for walleye, pike, and smallmouth bass. Eastern timber wolves roam the park, but rarely expose themselves to human eyes. In summer the **Rainy Lake Visitor Center** *(Minn. 11)* offers naturalist-guided trips, including boat trips *(218-286-5470. Fare)* to view eagles.

Trips to the **Kettle Falls Hotel**★ *(Ash River Trail. 218-374-4404 or 888-534-6835. May-Oct. and Dec.-March)* leave from the **Kabetogama Lake Visitor Center** *(Off US 53)* from mid-May through August. Only accessible by water, the restored hotel has served fishermen, loggers, and a cohort of backwoods eccentrics for almost a century (see sidebar this page). Hikers who travel to Quill, Shoepack, and other lakes can make arrangements at both Visitor Centers to use boats kept at the lakes, at no charge.

From Voyageurs, head south on US 53 and Minn. 73 toward the Mesabi Range, where the earliest great fortunes were made mining iron ore in the Great Lakes area. Though some mines still operate, the region is trying to transform itself into a tourist attraction, dubbed Iron Country. Just west of Chisholm, the **Ironworld Discovery Center** *(Off US 169. 218-254-3321. June–Labor Day; adm. fee)* is a blend of mining museum and amusement park. Perched above the defunct open-pit Glen Mine, it features exhibits on taconite mining and the immigrants who did the work, miniature golf that follows the stages of ore refining, big name concerts, and a tubular water slide.

In Chisholm's Memorial Park awaits a more traditional commemoration of mining heritage, the **Minnesota Museum of Mining** *(218-254-5543. Mem. Day–Labor Day; adm. fee).* Though the buildings show some wear, the museum has an extensive collection of climb-aboard mining equipment and a rambling miniature diorama of mountains, towns, trains, and mining operations by artist F.L. Jaques.

In the early 1900s, the town of **7** **Hibbing** *(Chamber of Commerce 218-262-3895 or 800-444-2246)* had to pick up and move as the Hull Rust Mahoning Mine pit ate its way into the downtown area. The best vantage for viewing the 3.5-mile pit is from the overlook at the **Hull Rust Mahoning Open Pit Iron Mine Visitor Center** *(3rd Ave. E. 218-262-4900. Mid-May–Sept.),* which has mining exhibits; you can view a blasting every Wednesday between 11 a.m. and noon. The site where the town once stood is surrounded on three sides by the pit, but its remains are still visible, with outdoor plaques explaining what was where, and photos of the big move. The **Greyhound Bus Origin Center** *(23rd St. and 5th Ave. E. 218-262-4166. Mid-May–mid-Sept.; adm. fee)* depicts the birth of the bus line here, and displays such relics as the snazzy 1931 White Bus.

Driving into **Eveleth** on US 53, keep an eye out for the "world's largest" hockey stick, a 107-footer that's hard to miss on Grant Street. The town is home to the **U.S. Hockey Hall of Fame** *(US 53 and Hat Trick Ave.*

Tiltin' Hilton

Even a teetotaler may lose balance walking around the pool table in the old loggers' saloon at the Kettle Falls Hotel. The historic hotel, deep in Voyageurs National Park and reachable only by watercraft, cheerfully provided illegal whiskey to loggers and fishermen during Prohibition. Hotel owner Bob Williams even supplemented his business by sending home-brew hooch down to St. Louis and Kansas City. But it's not the fumes from 70 years ago that will test your equilibrium in the Kettle Falls saloon today. Cold winter temperatures caused the rocks beneath the hotel to "heave," pushing up the center of the room, while spring runoff undermined the foundation around the edges, causing them to sag. The result is a floor as curved as the back of a barrel, and an inspired nickname, too: the "Tiltin' Hilton."

Street signs in Eveleth

218-744-5167. May-Nov. daily, Dec.-April Thurs.-Sat.; adm. fee), with exhibits on enshrined players, a big Zamboni machine, and a rink where you can take a slap shot.

Continue north to **Soudan Underground Mine State Park** ★ (Off Minn. 169. 218-753-2245. Mem. Day–Labor Day; tour and parking fees). After touring the engine house and crusher, visitors join a guide and hop aboard a rattling cage above the "skip," which carried the ore, and drop down one of Minnesota's oldest and deepest iron ore mine shafts.

Proceed east on Minn. 169 to ❽ **Ely,** a popular gateway to the **Boundary Waters Canoe Area Wilderness** ★ ★ (Permit Station, in International Wolf Center, 1396 Minn. 169. 218-365-7681. Advance permits 800-745-3399). The Boundary Waters has become almost too known for its own good; intensely managed access, and the stacks of canoes at every corner in Ely seem at times to belie the spirit of wilderness. Nevertheless, it remains the Xanadu of canoeists, nearly 200,000 of whom paddle amid its lakes and rivers each year. Permits can be secured up to nine months ahead; advance permits are recommended for holidays and in late summer. Rangers often suggest trips to some of the many lakes on the outskirts of the Boundary Waters, less restricted non-wilderness areas with similar scenery and fishing that, ironically, get less use.

136

Riding a wolf sculpture, International Wolf Center near Ely

Celebrated wolf biologist Dr. David Mech campaigned for the impressive **International Wolf Center** ★ (1396 Minn. 169. 218-365-4695 or 800-359-9653. May–mid-Oct. daily, mid-Oct.–April weekends; adm. fee). It features an exhibit on the mythology and natural history of wolves, arranged around a display of mounted wolves playing and making a kill. A small pack of live wolves can be observed through glass while a staffer explains pack dynamics.

Visitors primed for wolf howls will perhaps get lucky as they head east (with windows rolled down) through Superior National Forest on Minn. 1, a scenic, twisty route that links up with the North Shore at Tettegouche State Park.

Lake District

● 505 miles ● 2 to 4 days ● Summer

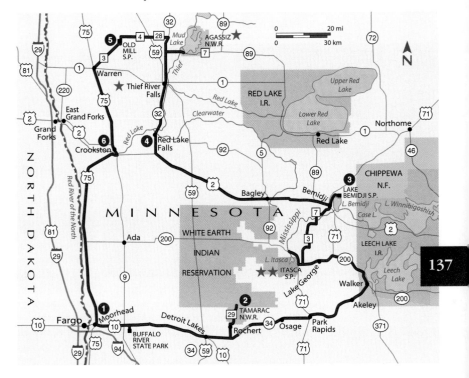

This is the beginning: the source of the greatest river system in North America, where you can wade across the headwaters of the Mississippi River and barely get your ankles wet (try that in Louisiana!). This part of Minnesota was once home to another phenomenon, Lake Agassiz. But you can search forever among the 15,291 lakes of Minnesota and not find it—because it's not there anymore. It was the granddaddy of 'em all, though; it covered much of Minnesota (and parts of North Dakota and Canada) during the waning of the last ice age.

The route explores the region that emerged when the glaciers melted and Lake Agassiz drained. From the beautiful Red River Valley at Moorhead, it travels east through woodlands jigsawed by lakes and streams to Lake Itasca, the Mississippi's source. After visiting Bemidji, it turns northwest, where the woods give way to grassy, windswept plains. Thinly populated, this corner of the state still has the open expanses of its homestead days. At Crookston the drive returns to the verdant Red River Valley, and it's time to get out the fishing poles.

Some think of **❶ Moorhead** *(Convention & Visitors Bureau 701-282-3653 or 800-235-7654)* as a poor cousin to Fargo, North Dakota, across the river, but it has its own distinguished past, displayed in the stately 1882 **Comstock House** *(506 8th St. 218-291-4211. Mem. Day–Sept. weekends; adm. fee).* Solomon Comstock made his wealth in land speculation along the new railroad lines. His daughter Ada Comstock became the

138

Tamarac National Wildlife Refuge

president of Radcliffe College. Near the Red River rises the tent roof of the **Heritage-Hjemkomst Interpretive Center** ★ *(202 1st Ave. N. 218-233-5604. Adm. fee),* peaking above the tall mast of a 76-foot Viking ship reproduction, built by the late Robert Asp. His children sailed it from Lake Superior to Norway in 1982; a film about this is shown at the center. On the lower level is the **Clay County Museum and Archives** *(218-233-4604),* with displays recounting the area's settlement.

Traveling east, you'll see the forests thicken, and lakes and marshes appear more frequently. It's habitat heaven, with migrating birds overhead and lakes swimming with walleye, pike, and bass. Hike among wildflowers or take a swim in the beach-lined pond at **Buffalo River State Park** *(Off US 10. 218-498-2124. Adm. fee).* Climb a ridge above the grasslands and you will be standing on the "beach" of ancient Lake Agassiz.

Proceed east on US 10, Minn. 34, and a short way north on County Road 29 to **❷ Tamarac National Wildlife Refuge** *(Cty. Rd. 29, N of Rochert. 218-847-2641),* where bald eagles and trumpeter swans are often spotted. As displays at the Visitor Center *(near jct. of Cty. Rd. 26 and Cty. Rd. 29)* illustrate, the refuge is a key migration stop for ducks and geese, and also provides a home for otters, deer, black bears, moose, and the rarely seen timber wolf. Note the swollen trunks of some trailside

maples: reminders that Ojibwe Indians once tapped syrup here, in addition to hunting, fishing, and gathering rice.

Farther east on Minn. 34, in the hills around **Osage,** you can follow tree-shaded boardwalks from one craftsperson's shop to another, watching blacksmiths, potters, and others at work at **Smoky Hills Artisan Community** *(1.5 miles W of Osage, on Minn. 34. 218-573-3300. Mem. Day–Labor Day; adm. fee).* Continue on to **Akeley,** legendary birthplace of Paul Bunyan. Here you'll find a prime photo op: You can pose recumbent in the hand of the (allegedly) biggest Paul Bunyan statue in the world. It stands in front of the **Akeley Paul Bunyan Museum** *(Minn. 34. 218-652-2369. Mem. Day–Labor Day),* which offers logging artifacts.

Continue to **Leech Lake,** and try not to be put off by its unfortunate name—or by the fact that locals in the lakeside town of **Walker** *(Chamber of Commerce 218-547-1313 or 800-833-1118)* hold an "ugly fish" festival every year. The eelpout sure isn't pretty, but it's honored with

Footbridge at the Mississippi headwaters, Itasca State Park

contests and races (such as the "Eelpout Peel-out"). Partially surrounded by Chippewa National Forest, the sprawling lake is lined with rustic resorts and private camps, and Walker offers fishing guide services *(call chamber).*

Now take Minn. 200 and US 71 northwest to **Itasca State Park**★★ *(East entrance off US 71. 218-266-2100. Adm. fee).* The location of the true headwaters of the Mississippi River was a controversy for three centuries before Henry Rowe Schoolcraft tromped through a thicket in northwestern Minnesota in 1832 (see sidebar this page). A short walk through the woods behind the Headwaters History Center is the lake's outlet, where the Mississippi begins its 2,350-mile journey to the Gulf of Mexico. Visitors can hike through the pines on this 32,000-acre preserve,

Mississippi Hunting

Explorers searched for the source of the Mississippi for centuries, and later clashed over whose patch of mud was the real thing. Henry Rowe Schoolcraft thought he'd settled it once and for all in 1832, when a Chippewa guide led him to a lake he later dubbed Itasca—a combination of Latin words meaning "true head." The Ojibwe, who had been there long before, called it Omushkos, meaning "elk," because of its shape. You might wonder about the smaller, higher lakes that drain into Itasca, such as little Nicollet Lake. Hydrologists counter that the source of a river system is a watershed, not the first, highest drip on the mountainside. Thus, Lake Itasca takes the prize. It is the gathering point for the uppermost basin in the Mississippi watershed, the place where the little tributaries pool and set out on the long journey to the Gulf of Mexico.

canoe its lakes, take a naturalist boat tour, and drive or bike a loop through its wilderness. Besides campgrounds, the park offers a lodge and cabins *(800-246-2267)*.

Now head to Bemidji on County Road 3 and County Road 7 (part of the Great River Road). On the Lake Bemidji shore stands a giant statue of Paul Bunyan and his blue ox, Babe *(Paul Bunyan Dr. and 3rd St. N.W.)*. Maybe, at 18 feet tall, this Bunyan is a miniature—remember, he used wagon wheels for buttons when he was one year old. Next to the statue is the **Tourist Information Center** *(218-751-3540 or 800-458-2223)*, where you can check out the massive Fireplace of States, built with stones from all around the country.

Now take County Road 21 and County Road 20 to reach ❸ **Lake Bemidji State Park** *(Cty. Rd. 20. 218-755-3843. Adm. fee)*. Here you can cross-country ski in winter, or ride snowmobiles on nearly 20 miles of groomed trails. During warmer months, visitors can walk the boardwalk through the bog, where orchids or insect-eating sundews are sometimes visible. The interpretive center explains the biology of the lake and shore, and offers guidance to trails such as Rocky Point.

Avid fishermen may want to detour up Minn. 89 onto the **Red Lake Indian Reservation** *(218-679-3341. Fishing mid-May–mid-Oct., permit required from Tribal Headquarters on Minn. 1, Red Lake)* to angle for trophy walleye. The forest thins and lakes are fewer as the route turns west on US 2 and then north toward the town of ❹ **Red Lake Falls** *(Visitor Information 218-253-2684)*. Driving the streets here you'll notice canoes and inner tubes all over the place. Tubes are the conveyance of choice on the high-bluffed Red Lake and Clearwater Rivers; just north of town, the outfitter Voyageurs View *(Cty. Rd. 13. 218-253-4329)* can provide equipment and shuttle service.

Paul Bunyan and Babe, Bemidji

Take Minn. 32 north to the town of **Thief River Falls** ★ *(Visitor Information 218-681-3720 or 800-827-1629)*. A statue of Chief Red Robe, a Chippewa who originally owned this land, stands at the junction of the Red Lake and Thief Rivers in Red Robe Park *(8th St. and Reserve)*. Flower gardens, recreation areas, and a fishing pier are also located in the park. A collection of historical buildings, including an 1908 schoolhouse and a 1939 sewer plant with 1860s artifacts, has been assembled at the **Peder Engelstad Pioneer Village** *(Oakland Park Rd. 218-681-5767. Mid-May–Labor Day Thurs.-Mon.; adm. fee)*.

Follow Minn. 32 north. Much of this country was cleared and drained for farms in the 19th century. The twilight glow on fields of wheat and sunflower is a beautiful sight, but you can glimpse the wilder past of this landscape at **Agassiz National Wildlife Refuge**★ *(Cty. Rd. 7. 218-449-4115. Headquarters open Mon.-Fri.)*, a 100-square-mile preserve of trees, cattails, and ponds that protects everything from herons to moose. Take a spin around the 4-mile auto tour *(closed in winter)*, walk the 0.25-mile **Mackstad Hiking Trail,** or obtain a key at the headquarters and climb the 100-foot observation tower. You'll see geese and ducks, and possibly a LeConte's sparrow. You might get a rare glimpse of an eastern gray wolf pack that roams this territory.

Backtrack to Minn. 32 and drive north to County Roads 28 and 4. West on County Road 4 brings you to

❺ Old Mill State Park *(Off Cty. Rd. 4. 218-437-8174)*, where you can see evidence of ancient Lake Agassiz in the ancient beach ridges formed as its shores receded. A flour mill erected by homesteaders in 1897 is fired up around Labor Day each year.

Nineteenth-century log cabin, Old Mill State Park

Take County Road 3 south to Warren. The **Marshall County Historical Museum** *(Fairgrounds, end of E. Johnson Ave. 218-745-4803. May–mid-Sept. Wed.-Fri.)* is a particularly good one, with a railroad depot, log cabin, and a series of storefronts that show how things were done a century ago.

There's good catfishing, as well as a fine array of late 19th-century buildings, in **❻ Crookston** *(Chamber of Commerce 218-281-4320)*, farther south on US 75. Some say you could hear the wheels of oxcarts from 6 miles away before the railroad era. You'll believe it when you see the huge cart in front of the **Polk County Museum** *(719 E. Roberts St. 218-281-1038. Mid-May–Sept.)*, which displays pioneer artifacts, farm machinery, and exhibits on Lake Agassiz.

Take US 75 south through farmlands to Moorhead.

● 485 miles ● 3 to 4 days ● Spring through autumn
● St. Paul Winter Carnival late Jan. to early Feb.

Putting St. Paul at the beginning of this journey, and, after a loop north and west, Minneapolis at the end, underlines the fact that there are real differences between them: The Twin Cities are fraternal, not identical. St. Paul is the older sibling, a trading post once known as "Pig's Eye" (a saloonkeeper's nickname), and now the dignified seat of state government. Minneapolis, on the other hand, became an industrial center when St. Anthony Falls was tapped to power saw- and flour mills in the 1840s, and it's the bigger, scrappier, more modern city today.

From St. Paul this route goes north and west to wind through forests, lakes, and rivers. It travels along the beautiful St. Croix Valley, loops around Mille Lacs Lake, then drops into the farm and granite-quarrying country around St. Cloud. After a stop at a living history farm, it's back to high-rise Minneapolis.

Before beginning your journey, visit the site from which the Twin Cities sprang. The bluffs at the juncture of the Mississippi and Minnesota Rivers were a smart choice in the 1820s for Americans to position a fort for policing the newly acquired Northwest Territory. This was a takeoff point for westward trade and expansion, and a reminder to lingering British and French interests of who was now in charge. Soldiers from **Fort Snelling** ★ *(Off Minn. 5. 612-726-1171. May-Oct.; adm. fee)* were the first to harness St. Anthony Falls for saw- and gristmills, and the fort became the locus of booming trade, missionary work, and community life. In the various buildings reconstructed around the diamond-shaped parade ground, locals play shopkeepers, blacksmiths, and other historical roles. From the fort towers you see a view of the rivers similar to the one a frontier sentry would have seen almost 200 years ago.

Aerial view of the Cathedral of St. Paul

143

The downtown area of ❶ **St. Paul** *(Convention & Visitors Bureau 612-297-6985 or 800-627-6101)* is compact enough that you can cover a lot of sights on foot, or take a 50-cent trolley *(Capital City Trolley 612-223-5600)* that stops at key places. Start just up the hill from the downtown area, where the Minnesota History Center, the state capitol, and the Cathedral of St. Paul dominate the skyline. The **Minnesota History Center** ★ *(345 Kellogg Blvd. W. 612-296-6126 or 888-727-8386)* contains exhibits on Native Americans and farming, as well as a research center. East along John Ireland Boulevard is the domed **State Capitol** ★ *(Aurora and Constitution Aves. 612-296-2881),* a monumental beaux arts structure of granite and marble, filled with statuary and murals. Head west on John Ireland Boulevard to see the **Cathedral of St. Paul** *(239 Selby Ave. 612-228-1766. Tours Mon., Wed., and Fri.),* an imposing 1915 French baroque church with a copper dome. Proceed west down what has historically been the city's most prestigious street, Summit Avenue, which runs along a bluff above the city. St. Paul boasts many extant 19th-century mansions, the most spectacular of

Bounty at Farmers' Market, St. Paul

which is the **James J. Hill House** ★ *(240 Summit Ave. 612-297-2555. Wed.-Sat.; adm. fee. Reservations recommended).* The Romanesque sandstone design is brooding and dark on the outside, but the ornate woodwork, chandeliers, and art gallery within indicate tasteful expenditure of the fortune Hill made from the Great Northern Railway.

Go down the hill by foot or drive to the mammoth **RiverCentre** *(7th St. and Kellogg Ave.),* a nearby cluster of museums and theaters; and **Lowertown** *(Bounded by I-94, Mississippi River, and Jackson St.),* the oldest downtown section, where spruced-up warehouses contain art studios and galleries, entertainment spots, and restaurants. Not far from the RiverCentre is the home of the acclaimed **St. Paul Chamber Orchestra** ★ *(Ordway Theater, 345 Washington St. 612-291-1144. Call for schedule),* which performs here and throughout the Twin Cities area with international guest soloists.

At the colorful **Minnesota Children's Museum** ★ *(10 W. 7th St. 612-225-6000. Mem. Day–Labor Day daily, Labor Day–Mem. Day Tues.-Sun.; adm. fee)* you can float a boat through a series of locks, sit on chairs made of recycled cardboard, and shift clouds around the ceiling on pulleys. Two blocks away stands the **Science Museum of Minnesota** ★ *(30 E. 10th St. 612-221-9444. Mem. Day–Labor Day daily, Labor Day–Mem. Day Tues.-Sun.; adm. fee),* where you can continue hands-on learning with a wave tank, a gravity well, and many more interactive displays. The museum has dinosaur and gem displays, and exhibits on little-known facets of Minnesota culture, such as the

lifestyle of Hmong refugees from Laos.

A couple of seasonal treats in St. Paul: Visitors in late January can catch the ice sculptures, parades, entertainment, and sports events at the popular, 10-day **St. Paul Winter Carnival** (*612-223-4700 or 800-488-4023. Late Jan.–early Feb.*). During warm months, veggies, honey, milk, and (occasionally) buffalo meat, all produced within a 50-mile radius, are among the offerings available from over 150 stalls at the downtown **Farmers' Market** (*290 E. 5th St. 612-227-6856. May-Oct. weekends*).

About a century ago, the tomatoes at the market might have come from the Gibbs family farm in nearby Falcon Heights. Costumed guides take visitors around the 7-acre **Gibbs Farm Museum**★ (*2097 W. Larpenteur Ave. 612-646-8629. May-Oct. Tues.-Sun.; adm. fee*), where they learn about quilting, candlemaking, and other farm stuff. Ask to hear the story of the matriarch, Jane DeBow (Gibbs), who grew up among the Dakota. Not far from the Gibbs' place is the **Como Zoo & Conservatory** (*1250 Kaufman Dr. 612-487-8200*), with a lake, walking and skiing trails, a Japanese garden, a conservatory, and, of course, the finned, feathered, and furry. For more of the same, try the **Minnesota Zoo** (*13000 Zoo Blvd., Apple Valley, 612-432-9000 or 800-366-7811. Adm. fee*), which creates spacious habitats for unusual species such as the Komodo dragon, and ferries visitors through caribou country by monorail (*fare*).

Boats at Taylors Falls

Now take I-94 and Minn. 95 to nearby ❷ **Stillwater**★ (*Chamber of Commerce 612-439-7700*), which can pull historical rank on the Twin Cities by noting that this was the site of the territorial convention in 1848. A century ago, it was the thriving timber industry along the St. Croix River that gave Stillwater its bustle; today, it's commuters and tourists, attracted by the small-town feel and the tin-sided and brick buildings packed along the riverside below the residential bluffs. You can huff up steep stone steps to look at the old mansions of the lumber barons, or ride the opensided **Stillwater Trolley** (*400 E. Nelson St.

612-430-0352. May-Oct., by reservation April and Nov.; fare) for a narrated tour.

Log booms no longer float down the St. Croix, but you can get some old-time flavor by riding the paddle wheeler **Empress Andiamo** *(Stillwater Municipal Dock, off Minn. 36. 612-430-1236. May-Oct.; fare. Reservations required)* for a scenic dinner cruise. You can also take a train ride along the river bluffs on the **Minnesota Zephyr**★ *(612-430-3000 or 800-992-6100. Call for schedule; fare. Reservations required),* which leaves from the **Stillwater Depot Logging and Railroad Museum** *(601 N. Main St.).* The latter houses an excellent photographic history of Stillwater in its lobby and a huge bateau (a canoelike boat used by trappers) hangs above the door. The three-hour trip on the *Zephyr* climbs west from the river along Brown's Creek, while passengers eat and drink in art deco dining cars.

Head north out of Stillwater and follow the **St. Croix National Scenic Riverway** *(Visitor Center, 117 S. Main St., Stillwater. 612-430-1938),* a favorite of canoeists. Minn. 95 runs along its west shore and stops in picturesque riverside hamlets, including the early logging town **Marine on St. Croix,** as well as **Scandia** and **Taylors Falls.** The water is peaceful below Taylors Falls, and canoeists can camp on islands and shorelines in designated zones between Stillwater and Marine on St. Croix.

146

Along the St. Croix National Scenic Riverway

Now take Minn. 95 and I-35 to **Pine City.** Native Americans and Europeans began bartering for beaver pelts in these parts as early as the 17th century, and a complex trading system emerged. The re-created ❸ **North West Company Fur Post** *(Cty. Rd. 7, 1.5 miles W of I-35. 320-629-6356. May–Labor Day Tues.-Sun.)* features actors playing the roles of traders, trappers, and Indian hunters.

Proceed west on County Road 7 to Minn. 70, and head north on Minn. 65. Soon you'll find a landscape of thick pine forest dotted with marshes, bogs, and lakes. Wild rice is abundant in these placid waters, and it is still harvested in the traditional way by Ojibwe at ❹ **Rice Lake National Wildlife Refuge**★ *(Minn. 65, 5 miles S of McGregor. 218-768-2402).* The refuge protects migrating ring-necked ducks, and nesting teal and Canada geese. Though you can't camp overnight, there are hiking and skiing trails, a wildlife-drive loop, and hunting and fishing areas.

A side trip south on US 169 leads to big, glacier-carved Mille Lacs Lake, and some insight into Ojibwe culture. The Ojibwe wrested this area away from the Dakota in the 18th century and still hold a small reservation along the lakeshore, site of the new **Mille Lacs Indian Museum** *(US 169 on lakeshore, N of Onamia. 320-532-3632. Adm. fee).* Dioramas depict traditional Ojibwe life, and programs and exhibits explain wild ricing, powwow dancing, and maple sugar production.

Famous for its walleye fishing, Mille Lacs Lake is home to resorts big and small, including the Indian-owned **Grand Casino Mille Lacs** *(777 Grand Ave., off US 169 near Onamia. 320-532-7777 or 800-626-5825),* which boasts golf, skiing, and top-notch restaurants. Gambling casinos owned by Indian tribes are doing big business in Minnesota, where 17 casinos are operated by Ojibwe or Dakota tribes.

For outdoor adventure in the area, there is the new **Soo Line** bicycle trail *(Cty. Rd. 26, Onamia to Isle),* and **Mille Lacs Kathio State Park** *(Cty. Rd. 26, 8 miles N of Onamia. 320-532-3523. Adm. fee),* with a 100-foot observation tower rising above the treetops, and lively canoeing *(call park for canoe rentals and bike outfitters)* on the Rum River between Shakopee and Ogechie Lakes.

147

Now drive south from Brainerd on Minn. 371 to the **Minnesota Military Museum** *(47th Infantry Division Rd., Bldg. 1-1. 320-632-7374. Mem. Day–Labor Day Wed.-Sun.),* which tells the stories of Minnesota residents who served in all military branches from the Civil War through the Persian Gulf conflict.

Snowshoes and skates, Charles A. Lindbergh House

Continue to ❺ **Little Falls,** home of Charles Lindbergh, who made history in 1927 when he crossed the Atlantic in a solo flight. He spent his summers on the Mississippi River and managed a family farm during his high school years. As a boy, Lindbergh slept on the screened porch of the **Charles A. Lindbergh House** *(1200 Lindbergh Dr. S. 320-632-3154. May–Labor Day daily, Labor Day–Oct. weekends; adm. fee),* which contains furnishings from the period Lindbergh lived here—1906 to 1920. An adjacent History Center contains exhibits on Lindbergh and his family.

Transportation up and down the Mississippi River was interrupted by St. Anthony Falls at Minneapolis. Since the

Sinclair Lewis

A side trip west to Sauk Centre is a must for fans of author Sinclair Lewis (1885-1951). This is the hamlet that inspired, if that's the word, the fictional town of Gopher Prairie, depicted with such ripping satire in his 1920 novel, *Main Street*. Born in Sauk Centre, Lewis was the son of a country doctor.

His credits include *Elmer Gantry, Dodsworth, Babbit,* and other acerbic portrayals of middle America. Though he refused a Pulitzer Prize for *Arrowsmith* in 1926, he did accept a Nobel Prize in 1930. You can visit the **Sinclair Lewis Boyhood Home** *(Sinclair Lewis Ave., 3.5 blocks W of Main St. 320-352-5359. Mem. Day–Labor Day; adm. fee)*, as well as the **Sinclair Lewis Museum** *(1220 S. Main St. 320-352-5201. Mem. Day–Labor Day daily, Labor Day–Mem. Day Mon.-Fri.)*.

section of river north of the falls offered clear sailing as far as ❻ **Sauk Rapids** and **St. Cloud,** the area became a trade center for local farms. Agriculture is still an economic mainstay, and visitors can see the productivity of the rich soil along the winding paths at **Munsinger Gardens**★ *(Riverside Park, Riverside Dr. S., St. Cloud. 320-255-7238)*. The park stretches along the river's east side and includes the Virginia Clemens Rose Garden, with over 1,000 rosebushes. Historical exhibits about the St. Cloud area are on display at the modern **Stearns County Heritage Center** *(235 S. 33rd Ave., St. Cloud. 320-253-8424. Adm. fee)*.

Now take US 10 southeast to **Elk River.** Anyone with farming roots knows about the Grange—an organization for farmers that became a powerful national force in the late 19th century. Its founder was Oliver H. Kelley, and his former abode is now a showcase for 19th-century farm life. Visitors can take the reins of a horse-drawn plough at the **Oliver H. Kelley Farm**★ *(15788 Kelley Farm Rd. 612-441-6896. May-Oct. Tues.-Sun., Visitor Center only daily; adm. fee)*, or learn other skills and handicrafts.

The tour's final stop, ❼ **Minneapolis**★★ *(Visitors Association 612-348-7000)* is the cultural heart of Minnesota, wedding a vibrant arts scene with careful preservation of its mid-19th-century roots. St. Anthony Falls was the engine of its growth—powering giant mills that ground the wheat of surrounding farms into flour. The falls has been chastened by a dam and power plant, but the big mills, grain silos, and warehouses are still in place. You can view them from a riverbank walking-and-biking path, the **Mississippi Mile**★ *(St. Anthony Falls Historic District, 125 Main St. S.E. 612-627-5433 or 800-445-7412. Guided tours May-Oct. Wed.-Sun.)*, between the downtown area and the river. Visitors can observe boats going through

Hubert H. Humphrey Metrodome, Minneapolis

the locks by the falls at Upper St. Anthony Lock and Dam and walk beneath the massive stone arches of the Historic **Stone Arch Bridge** *(Main St. S.E. and 6th Ave. S.E.)*. The downtown is pedestrian friendly, with the auto-free **Nicollet Mall** *(Nicollet Ave. bet. 3rd and 12th Sts.)* full of life and music during the summer, and 61 skyways that allow people to walk through a network of enclosed walkways without suffering the sting of harsh winter weather.

History buffs should start their Minneapolis tour at **Minnehaha Park** *(Minnehaha Pkwy. and Minn. 55)*, where you can walk or bike winding paths for a view of Minnehaha Falls (the inspiration for parts of Longfellow's *Song of Hiawatha*) and visit one of the oldest surviving houses in Minneapolis, the 1850 **John H. Stevens House** *(4901 Minnehaha Ave. 612-722-2220. Mid-May–Sept. Fri.-Sun.; adm. fee)*, a modest white clapboard house with period furnishings and exhibits on the city's history. The **American Swedish Institute**★ *(2600 Park Ave. 612-871-4907. Closed Mon.; adm. fee)* was founded in 1909 by Swan J. Turnblad, a self-made millionaire whose châteauesque mansion is adorned with carved wood paneling, decorative ceilings, and Swedish porcelain tile stoves. The museum displays furnishings and provides classes, lectures, music programs, and a research archive.

149

The **Minneapolis Institute of Arts**★★ *(2400 3rd Ave. S. 612-870-3131. Closed Mon. Tours available)* rotates exhibits from its enormous holdings—ranging from 11th-century B.C. Chinese bronze work to Rembrandt canvases and photographs of Marilyn Monroe. A busy schedule of classes, lectures, and films for all ages goes nonstop.

Art lovers with a taste for the cutting edge will gravitate to the **Walker Art Center**★ *(725 Vineland Pl. 612-375-7622. Closed Mon.; adm. fee)*, a busy hub of art,

Contrasting architecture, downtown Minneapolis

dance, music, and film. In a given week, visitors may tour the absurdist Dada creations of Duchamp or construct their own postcards in a workshop. Across the street lies the Walker's free and wondrous **Minneapolis Sculpture Garden**★★, perhaps best known for Claes Oldenburg's giant "Spoonbridge and Cherry." The emphasis is modern, and the pieces divvied up among hedged "galleries" are wonderfully varied. Also adjacent to the Walker is the **Guthrie Theater**★ *(Vineland Pl. 612-377-2224 or 800-848-4912. Performances Tues.-Sun.; adm. fee)*, one of the country's most renowned regional theaters. Its adjunct, **Guthrie, Too** *(700 N. 1st St. 612-377-2224)* lies in the Northern Warehouse district and serves up experimental fare.

Southeast Ramble

● 585 miles ● 3 to 4 days ● Spring through autumn
● Apple blossoms in spring

If the North Woods of Minnesota are a land of lakes, the southeastern corner is a region of rivers. The Mississippi River was a great conduit of commerce in the 19th century—a liquid highway ferrying goods and settlers to its surrounding lands. A rich river culture soon thrived along the mighty river's banks and tributaries, as well as those of the Minnesota River, which cuts a V shape across the state's southern part.

This loop begins along the Apple Blossom Scenic Drive, north of La Crescent, and on to the Great River Road, where pavement follows paddle wheelers.

Bluff above the Mississippi River, along Apple Blossom Scenic Drive

It touches the fringe of the sprawling Minneapolis metropolitan area (see page 142) for some self-indulgent fun at the Mall of America, then heads west to the site of the 1862 Dakota conflict. After journeying west to Native American history sites, the route returns to the Mississippi River by a southerly route through rich farm country.

Take Elm Street north out of ❶ **La Crescent** *(Chamber of Commerce 507-895-2800 or 800-926-9480)* and follow the signs for a spin on the **Apple Blossom Scenic Drive.** Spectacular limestone bluffs carved by the Mississippi River are visible from the Minnesota banks. Stop at the well-marked overlook on County Road 1 for a view of the wide, winding river. Much of the surrounding habitat is part of the **Upper Mississippi River National Wildlife and Fish Refuge** ★ *(507-452-4232)*, which has protected wildlife along the river since 1924. In the autumn, stop at **Leidel's Apple Orchard** *(Cty. Rd. 1, 3 miles N of La Crescent. 507-895-4832 or 507-895-8221)* to learn why La Crescent calls itself the Apple Capital of Minnesota.

Proceed northwest on US 61 and the **Great River Road.** When steamboats plied this river there were no dams, just treacherous shifting sandbars. The average life of a riverboat was only about five years—it would either run aground or explode. But these boats were

Apple orchard country, near La Crescent

151

ten times as fast as wagons, and they thrived on the river until the coming of railroads. One of the last of the wooden-hulled steamboats has been rebuilt and docked in concrete in **Winona** *(Chamber of Commerce 507-452-2272 or 800-657-4972)*. The **Julius C. Wilkie Steamboat Center** *(Main St. at Levee Park. 507-454-1254. Mem. Day–Labor Day Tues.-Sun.; adm. fee)* features displays on river history, and a plush Victorian salon on its second floor. These days, steamboats on the river, such as the **Winona Island Princess** *(Tour boat center, 2 Johnson St. 507-457-0979. May–mid-Oct. Wed.-Sun.; fare. Reservations recommended)*, ferry sightseers.

Continue north to another river town, **Wabasha,** where the oldest operating hotel in Minnesota, the charming redbrick **Anderson House** *(333 W. Main St. 612-565-4524)*, offers feline bed warmers—cats—to the nonallergic. Towns along the Mississippi trying to regain the vibrancy of steamboat days should emulate ❷ **Red Wing** ★ *(Chamber of Commerce 612-388-4719)*,

Mammoth Mall

A trip to the **Mall of America** doesn't just entail shopping: It's also a chance to ride a roller coaster, play miniature golf, get married, and shoot some hoops. The centerpiece of the Mall is **Knott's Camp Snoopy** (612-883-8600), a 7-acre, family theme park crammed with entertainment possibilities—a carousel, Ferris wheel, and Paul Bunyan's Log Chute, among many others. At the **Oshman's Supersports USA** (612-854-9444) sporting goods store, shoppers can tee off, rollerblade, and take batting practice. More than 1,200 couples have tied the knot at the **Chapel of Love** (612-299-5683), which seats 75. And don't forget the **LEGO Imagination Center** (612-858-8949), with giant models made of LEGO bricks, including a dinosaur. The store allows visitors to play with piles of LEGO pieces at no charge.

where local industries, from agriculture to shipping, underpin a picturesque historical facade. The town's story is told in exhibits at the hilltop **Goodhue County Historical Museum** ★ (*1166 Oak St. 612-388-6024. Closed Mon.; adm. fee*), where you can pick up a printed guide to the downtown and residential historic districts. One of the largest employers in town, the Red Wing Shoe Company, has restored several Main Street buildings, including the elegant, Victorian **St. James Hotel** (*406 Main St. 612-388-2846*).

Now turn west on Minn. 19 to the hamlet of **Cannon Falls** (*Chamber of Commerce 507-263-2289*). Here you can hike and bike the 19.7-mile Cannon Valley Trail or paddle your canoe along the **Cannon River** (*call chamber for information on bike rentals and canoe outfitters*). The trail parallels the river in places, which winds along farmlands, gorges, and good fishing reservoirs (you have to portage around the dams). The Minnesota Department of Natural Resources (*612-296-5029*) provides maps to canoe this relatively easy float.

Travel north on Minn. 20 and US 61 toward Hastings, and the **Carpenter Nature Center** (*12805 Cty. Rd. 21, off US 10. 612-437-4359*), a peaceful retreat of 600 acres along the St. Croix River, just above its junction with the Mississippi. The center provides environmental education programs in reconstructed prairie and oak savanna habitats. Visitors can picnic in a tree-shaded gazebo, or hike down to a sandy beach on the river.

For a dive into the country's largest mall, take US 10/61, and I-494 to the outskirts of the Twin Cities and the enormous ❸ **Mall of America** ★ (*I-494 and Minn. 77, Bloomington. 612-883-8800*). Unveiled in 1992 with great fanfare, the mall features hundreds of shops, as well as 25 restaurants, a movie theater, nightclubs, and scads of entertainment possibilities (see sidebar this page). It's not the biggest mall in the world—but it takes 12,000 employees to run it. With a school, a wedding chapel, and a dental clinic, it's practically a world unto itself. You can shop till you drop, or just gawk at specialty shops such as FAO Schwarz, whose Barbie Boutique even sells Barbie clothes for human children. Guilt-ridden mall rats can make this an educational experience by riding a conveyor sidewalk through the basement **UnderWater World** ★ (*612-883-0202. Adm. fee*), a 1.2-million-gallon aquarium that whisks visitors on a journey from the Minnesota headwaters to the Caribbean Sea.

Resisting the gravitational pull of the Twin Cities (see page 142, "Twin Cities and Beyond"), head southwest on US 169 and Minn. 19, into the verdant farmlands of the Minnesota River Valley. This is the site of one of the bloodiest conflicts between Native Americans and settlers. The Dakota unsuccessfully resisted settlers' attempts to curtail their nomadism and force them to farm. In 1862,

LEGO Imagination Center, Mall of America, Bloomington

after crop failures and tardy government rations, young warriors rebelled. Whites and Indians battled up and down the valley, with hundreds of lives lost on both sides. The story is told at the ❹ **Lower Sioux Agency State Historic Site** *(7 miles E of Redwood Falls, off Cty. Rd. 19. 507-697-6321. May-Oct.; adm. fee),* where a stone warehouse from the 19th century still stands.

Turn south onto US 71 and drive through the grassy plains where Indians once followed bison herds. Bison and other creatures are depicted in over 2,000 Native American quartzite stone carvings at **5** **Jeffers Petroglyphs**★ *(Off Cty. Rd. 10, 35 miles S of Redwood Falls. 507-697-6321. May–Labor Day Fri.-Sun.).*

Backtrack on US 14 and rejoin the Minnesota River at **New Ulm** *(Chamber of Commerce 507-354-4217 or 888-463-9856),* which was the site of the second skirmish in the U.S.-Dakota Conflict of 1862 (see sidebar this page). The exhibits at the **Brown County Museum**★ *(2 N. Broadway. 507-354-2016. April-Oct. daily, Nov.-March Mon.-Sat.; adm. fee)* tell the story of the battle, and artifacts from early German colonists are displayed. The **August Schell Brewing Company** *(Schell's Park, off 18th St. 507-354-5528. Mem. Day–Labor Day; adm. fee)* dates back to before the conflict and is still producing beer. Visitors can tour the gardens, brewery, and museum.

Continue east, along US 14, to Owatonna's **Village of Yesteryear** *(1448 Austin Rd. 507-451-1420. May-Sept. Tues.-Sun.; adm. fee),* a collection of antique-laden buildings assembled into a late 19th-century farm town. A schoolhouse, church, general store, and blacksmith shop display old wares and offer occasional demonstrations.

Farther east along US 14 lies **6** **Rochester** *(Chamber of Commerce 507-288-4331 or 800-634-8277),* where Dr. William Worrall Mayo started a small-town practice in 1863. His two sons later joined him and eventually they built the **Mayo Clinic.** The legendary Mayo operates clinics throughout the country, but its nerve center remains the Rochester "campus," a cluster of clinics, laboratories, and two busy hospitals. Free tours begin at the **Mayo Building** *(200 1st St. S.W. 507-284-9258),* and

Remembering the Dakota

Little did the German settlers know what was in store when they staked land on the edge of the Minnesota River to found New Ulm in 1854. Eight years later, during the U.S.-Dakota Conflict, hundreds of settlers staved off fierce attacks by the Native Americans, who had just overtaken the Lower Sioux Agency, 40 miles northwest. Though more than 300 of the Dakota were sentenced to hang, President Abraham Lincoln commuted 265 of the death sentences; the remaining 38 were executed the day after Christmas 1862, in **Mankato** *(25 miles E of New Ulm).* The execution is noted with a plaque at Front and Main Streets.

include a visit to the 1928 Plummer Building, with ornate balconies and statuary. One of the Mayo sons, Charles, built the 50-room **Historic Mayowood Mansion** *(3720 Mayowood Rd. S.W. 507-282-9447. May-Oct., call for schedule; adm. fee)*, which is decorated with furniture and art collected by the Mayos.

Take US 63 south and Minn. 16 east, through hilly farm country and stop at **Forestville/Mystery Cave State Park** *(Off Cty. Rd. 5. 507-352-5111)*, a favorite of equestrians. Part of the south branch of the Root River has carved out an underground labyrinth: At Mystery Cave *(507-937-3251. Adm. fee)*, visitors can walk through a network of passages punctuated with pools of water and a decorative backdrop of etched limestone.

Return to La Crescent via Minn. 16.

155

Sailboat race along the Mississippi River

For More Information

ILLINOIS
Illinois Bureau of Tourism 312-744-2400 or 800-226-6632.
Department of Natural Resources, Office of Public Services Hunting and fishing licenses, state parks and campground information 217-782-7454.
Department of Transportation Road conditions 800-452-4368.

INDIANA
Indiana Division of Tourism 317-232-8860 or 800-469-4612.
Department of Transportation Road conditions 317-232-5533.
Division of Fish and Wildlife Hunting and fishing license information 317-232-4080.
Division of State Parks and Reservoirs State parks and campground information 317-232-4124.

OHIO
Ohio Department of Travel and Tourism 800-BUCKEYE.
Department of Natural Resources, Public Information Center State parks and campground information 614-265-6791.
Division of Wildlife Hunting and fishing license information 614-265-6300.
State Highway Patrol Weather and road conditions 888-264-7623 (Ohio and bordering states only).

MICHIGAN
Michigan Travel Bureau 800-543-2937.
AAA Michigan Broadcast News Line Road conditions 800-337-1334.
AAA Michigan Broadcast News Line Road conditions 800-337-1334.
Department of Natural Resources Hunting and fishing license information 517-373-1204.
Parks and Recreation Division State parks and campground information 517-373-9900. Campground reservations 800-44-PARKS.

WISCONSIN
Wisconsin Dept. of Tourism 800-372-2737 or 608-266-2161.
Bureau of Parks and Recreation State parks and campground information 608-266-2181.
Department of Natural Resources, Bureau of Customer Service and Licensing Hunting and fishing license information 608-266-2621.
State Highway Patrol Road conditions 800-762-3947 (Wis. and bordering states only).

MINNESOTA
Minnesota Office of Tourism 612-296-5029.
Department of Natural Resources, License Bureau Hunting and fishing license information 612-296-4506.
Department of Transportation Road conditions 800-542-0220.
Division of Parks and Recreation State parks and campground information 612-296-6157. Campground reservations 800-246-2267.

HOTEL & MOTEL CHAINS
(Accommodations in all six states unless otherwise noted)
Best Western International 800-528-1234
Budget Host 800-BUD-HOST
Choice Hotels 800-4-CHOICE
Clarion Hotels 800-CLARION (except Minn., Wis.)
Comfort Inns 800-228-5150
Courtyard by Marriott 800-321-2211
Days Inn 800-325-2525
Doubletree Hotels 800-222-TREE (except Wis.)
Econo Lodge 800-446-6900
Embassy Suites 800-362-2779
Hampton Inn 800-HAMPTON
Hilton Hotels 800-HILTONS
Holiday Inns 800-HOLIDAY
Howard Johnson 800-654-2000
Hyatt Hotels and Resorts 800-233-1234
Marriott Hotels Resorts Suites 800-228-9290
Motel Six 800-466-8356
Quality Inns-Hotels-Suites 800-228-5151
Radisson Hotels Intl. 800-333-3333
Ramada Inns 800-2-RAMADA
Red Roof Inns 800-843-7663
Ritz-Carlton 800-241-3333 (Mich. and Ohio only)
ITT Sheraton Hotels 800-325-3535 (except Ind.)
Super 8 Motels 800-843-1991
Travelodge International, Inc. 800-255-3050
Utell International 800-223-9868

ILLUSTRATIONS CREDITS
Photographs in this book are by Layne Kennedy, except the following: 11, Gail Mooney; 14, Gail Mooney; 38, Karen Keeney; 42, Ron McQueeney/IMS Photo; 54-55, Richard A. Cooke, III; 78, Michigan State Sports Information; 99, Bob Sacha; 112, Jim Koepnick/EAA; 118, Zane Williams/Tony Stone Images; 127, John & Ann Mahan; 134, Matt Bradley; 148, Minnesota Twins Baseball Club.

NOTES ON AUTHOR AND PHOTOGRAPHER
GEOFFREY O'GARA is a freelance writer and documentary television producer based in Lander, Wyoming. He wrote a book on his travels around America with the 1930s WPA guides, and is currently finishing a book about the Wind River in Wyoming. He is a contributing editor to National Geographic TRAVELER and contributes to various guidebooks for the National Geographic Society.

Son of an Air Force pilot, LAYNE KENNEDY grew up traveling the United States. His first camera, purchased at age five for $2, didn't produce any memorable results, but did illuminate the magic of the medium. Trained in fine art photography, he is known for editorial photography that conveys a strong sense of place. His images appear in *Smithsonian, LIFE, Audubon, Islands, Sports Illustrated, Backpacker,* and other magazines. He has contributed to many books for several publishers, including National Geographic, North-Word Press, and Voyageur Press.

Index

160

Composition for this book by the National Geographic Society Book Division. Printed and bound by R.R. Donnelley & Sons, Willard, Ohio. Color separations by Digital Color Image, Pensauken, New Jersey. Paper by Consolidated/Alling & Cory, Willow Grove, Pennsylvania. Cover printed by Miken Companies, Inc. Cheektowaga, New York.

Library of Congress CIP Data
O'Gara, Geoffrey.
  Great Lakes / by Geoffrey O'Gara ; photographed by Layne Kennedy.
      p. cm.—(National Geographic's driving guides to America)
  Includes index.
  ISBN 0-7922-3432-4
  1. Great Lakes Region—Tours. 2. Automobile travel—Great Lakes Region—Guidebooks. I. Title. II. Series.
  F551.039 1997
  917.704'33—dc21   97-33681
                                                              CIP

Visit the Society's Web site at www.nationalgeographic.com.